The subject of the tripartite n  stood by very many. Yet, I am c tial keys to full maturation in t. has not only found a key to understanding this issue, but he has also turned the key to open a door that is as vast and panoramic as one's spiritual eyes can see. I believe *Thrones of Our Soul* will help us better understand what the apostle Peter meant when he wrote that we are "partakers of the divine nature."

—JOHN PAUL JACKSON
STREAMS MINISTRIES

In his simple yet powerful writing style, Paul Keith Davis does in this book what many neglect to do when authoring what the Lord is saying to the church. In *Thrones of Our Soul*, Paul Keith is teaching the literal Scriptures, the very truths taught by Christ Himself as to what it means to walk the Christian life in these last days. These very things you will read are those that most offended the religious men of the day and caused them to be so filled with hate that they would partner with Satan himself to crucify our Lord.

How could the Christian walk be so simple and yet so profoundly different than what we would do, when left to our own understanding?

Jesus Christ is speaking to the Church in this hour about his kingdom and the very principles that will cause it to grow, flourish and powerfully change the world.

Intimacy. Humility. Servanthood. Preferring one another. Becoming a habitation for the Lord Himself. The most radical ideas that the world has ever been taught and the opposite of the "teachings" of the "Prince of the power of the air."

May the Church grasp fully what God is showing to Paul Keith Davis in this hour. It can't be said that what Paul Keith is teaching is new. It can be said that what he has been shown by the Holy Spirit about the kingdom of God is revolutionary to the core.

—STEVE SHULTZ
THE ELIJAH LIST
WWW.ELIJAHLIST.COM

I count it a great honor to be able to endorse Paul Keith's book. I've had the privilege of knowing Paul Keith and his wife, Wanda, for over a decade now. We have ministered in numerous conferences.

Paul Keith Davis has been called to the kingdom for such a time as this. His burning passion for Christ's kingdom has brought him to a deep and intimate walk with Christ Jesus. This book will help you prepare to advance in your walk with Christ. You too will hunger for the establishing of God's truth and righteousness. It is most evident that here is a man who has spent years building a close relationship with the Holy Spirit. He is a man after God's heart and a man in whom there is a pure heart and honest motives. This book will be a great help and blessing to all who are desperately seeking to advance in their call to know more about the prophetic destiny to which they were born.

Paul Keith and his wife, Wanda, are some of the purest, most noble people I know. Your heart will be blessed and your life radically changed by the insights released in this excellent book. With great honor I fully recommend this excellent book.

—BOBBY CONNER
DEMONSTRATION OF GOD'S POWER MINISTRIES
BOX 1028
MORAVIAN FALLS, NC 28654
WWW.BOBBYCONNER.ORG

Thrones of Our Soul is a clarion call to the thirsty believer who wants to be drawn into the heart of God. If you want to go behind the veil and discover some of the King's hidden secrets then you will need to eat at such a banquet table that Paul Keith has prepared. The contents of this book contain open revelations from God Himself. It is much more than a glimpse into the secret places; it is also a full view on how to become an overcomer. You will find within the pages of this book why Paul Keith walks in Christlikeness. I have been stirred by his life and now I am stirred by his book.

—JOSEPH SCHUCHERT

THRONES OF OUR SOUL

THRONES OF OUR SOUL

PAUL KEITH DAVIS

CREATION
HOUSE PRESS.

THRONES OF OUR SOUL by Paul Keith Davis
Published by Creation House Press
A Part of Strang Communications Company
600 Rinehart Road
Lake Mary, FL 32746
www.creationhouse.com

Unless otherwise noted, the Scripture quotations are from the New American Standard Bible. Copyright © 1960, 1962, 1963, 1968, 1971, 1972, 1973, 1975, 1977 by the Lockman Foundation. Used by permission.

Scripture quotations marked NKJV are from the New King James Version of the Bible. Copyright © 1979, 1980, 1982 by Thomas Nelson, Inc., publishers. Used by permission.

Scripture quotations marked KJV are from the King James Version of the Bible.

Library of Congress Control Number: 2003104685
International Standard Book Number: 1-59185-233-1

03 04 05 06 07 — 8 7 6 5 4 3 2 1
Printed in the United States of America

ACKNOWLEDGMENTS

I would be extremely amiss if I did not initially acknowledge, with sincere thanks and affection, my wife and fortifying support, Wanda. The fingerprint of her insight and wisdom can be discovered throughout the book. I would also like to express my appreciation to my children, Annah, Caleb, Natalie, Scott and Bridgett, and to my family for the strong support and words of encouragement.

Nick and Bonnie Burkardt and Joe and Karalyn Schuchert have faithfully stood with Wanda and me in this endeavor providing loyal friendship and devoted affirmation. For that we are notably grateful.

It has been my great privilege to have two men of considerable anointing and gifting as mentors and friends. They are Bob Jones and Bobby Conner. It was divine favor that allowed the many years of encouragement and impartation from them and the bond of commitment and fraternal affection that binds us together. They each share in the fruit of this ministry and the things the Lord is able to achieve to His glory.

Many thanks to Bill Lancaster for help with edits and advice and also Steve Kenney and our friends at Kodiak Community Church for their generous support.

We would also like to acknowledge the many prayer supporters and followers of our ministry who read our material and often send words of encouragement and blessing. We believe the Lord is providing a strong intercessory base to pave the way through prayer for insight with understanding and is assigning warriors essential in the battle we are being commissioned to engage.

Blessings to all.

TABLE OF CONTENTS

INTRODUCTION

To gaze directly into the face of God and, like Adam, walk with Him in the "cool of the day" without shame or reservation—this is our high calling and lofty mandate for this hour. It is staggering to the natural mind to contemplate such a virtuous ideal. Nevertheless, it is God's intent to find a body of believers in whom He can take full possession of their spirit, soul and body to accomplish kingdom purposes on the earth.

There are a number of scriptures often quoted and embraced in our noble pursuit to be anointed for ministry. Likewise, throughout the Church, there are many much-needed equipping ministries dedicated to teaching Christians how to walk in the anointing of God's power for ministry.

These vital ministries teach Christians how to know God's grace for the gifts of the Spirit, for prophesy, for healing, for ministering salvation and deliverance to hurting and needy people. The Scriptures clearly express that we should earnestly and zealously desire spiritual gifts.

Nonetheless, as once said, "The main thing is to keep the main thing, the main thing." That is, to know Him intimately and affectionately and walk in the full measure of His provision for our generation.

Clearly, we are living at the dawning of a new day, and the Word of Truth is coming alive within the hearts of radically desperate saints who are setting their faces like flint to achieve the heavenly mandate and high calling established for our generation.

1

Peter, John and Paul were considered pillars of the early Church who highlighted the revelation of the Word for their day. They presented to the people the anointed promises and spiritual reality available to them. We also should be like the Bereans and study the Scriptures to determine the revelation of His Word for our day and the long-foretold promises for the righteous generation.

The nobility of the Bereans

The Bereans were described as a noble group, inasmuch as they readily received the Spirit of Truth working through Paul and Silas *and* they searched the Scriptures to affirm their message in the written Word. Paul delivered "cutting-edge" truth that was contradictory to the previous understanding of the Scriptures taught by the leaders of that day.

> **The brethren immediately sent Paul and Silas away by night to Berea, and when they arrived, they went into the synagogue of the Jews. Now these were more noble-minded than those in Thessalonica, for they received the word with great eagerness, examining the Scriptures daily [to see] whether these things were so.**
> **—Acts 17:10–11**

Even so, Paul's message was securely established in the written Word and conferred the true application of the Scriptures concerning the promised Messiah and the kingdom of God. This is the virtuous example we should likewise follow.

> **Be diligent to present yourself approved to God as a workman who does not need to be ashamed, accurately handling the word [*logos*] of truth.**
> **—2 Timothy 2:15**

By diligently studying the Scriptures, the Bereans were

able to fully appropriate their faith in the message of truth presented through Paul and enter into its reality. Although the kingdom message entrusted to Paul was unprecedented and foreign to previous understanding, it was truth and the message of the hour as their inheritance. The same Spirit is being deposited today to establish the message of truth for our day and the grace to walk in it.

Charles Spurgeon once spoke of the *logos* saying, "So, brethren, especially is it with the Incarnate Word. We are in the habit of calling the Bible the Word of God. I suppose that is accurate enough . . . of this incarnate Word, this everlasting Logos, we may say that he standeth for ever. Jesus Christ, the same yesterday, today and forever."[1] The Bible is not simply the Word of God; it is the revelation of Jesus Christ.

Therefore, our quest is not simply to acquire knowledge but to know the Living Truth and walk in the full revelation of the Lord Jesus Christ. This position of spiritual enlightenment transcends ministry and finds its origin in relationship with Him.

With that view in focus, we must invest ourselves to find the place of intimate exchange and sacred fellowship with the Lord and be completely unwilling to compromise that relationship for any purpose. Notice the heart's cry of the apostle Paul, even after many years of powerful ministry, his passionate desire was "to know Him, and the power of His resurrection and the fellowship of His sufferings" (Philippians 3:10).

Those who know their God

There is an imperative spiritual reality we must not allow ourselves to divert from if we are to become the royal priesthood and holy nation promised in Scripture. The prophet Daniel foretold a period of great hardship and spiritual darkness that would permeate a generation known as "the

time of the end." Yet, in the midst of the darkness that
would cover the earth and the people, there would be a company who:

> . . . *know their God* [and] shall be strong, and carry
> out great exploits.
> —DANIEL 11:32 (NKJV, EMPHASIS ADDED)

Very often we emphasize the latter portion of this verse
concerning the manifestation of mighty exploits and power.
Residing within many is the yearning desire to "display
strength and take action" and witness great demonstrations
of the Spirit and power. However, the most important aspect
of this notable prophetic promise is to know Him: to know
our God intimately and affectionately, and through that
relationship do mighty exploits for His glory.

The insight of Moses

Exodus 33 describes the directive of God to occupy the
Land of Promise following the deliverance of Israel at the
hand of Moses from the bondage and oppression of Egypt.
The covenant people of God were imminently facing the
inheritance of their promises, thus providing a perfect typi-
cal scenario for today's generation of the Church.

Many within the Church are presently positioned to
inherit countless wonderful promises. Some have been called
to a ministry of healing, and that promise for the healing
anointing is at the door. Others perhaps have been called to
a prophetic ministry, and the revelatory gifts are in view; the
promises of God are on the horizon. Even so, Moses identified the greater purpose in verses 15 and 16:

> Then he said to Him, "If Your presence does not go
> with us do not lead us up from here. For how then can
> it be known that I have found favor in Your sight, I and

Your people? Is it not by Your going with us, so that we, I and Your people, may be distinguished from all the other people who are upon the face of the earth?"
—EXODUS 33:15–16

Although Moses delivered Israel to the threshold of inheriting their wonderful and great promises, he nonetheless pleaded with God not to lead them from that place if His presence did not accompany them. Otherwise, how were they to be distinguished from the other nations on the earth?

Other nations, such as Moab under the hired leadership of Balaam, were evidently offering sacrifices and performing religious duties in the same manner as Israel. However, one notable difference separated the two nations: A cloud by day and pillar of fire by night accompanied Israel, representing the manifest presence of God.

It is in knowing Him and abiding in His presence that we will be distinguished from among the people and belief systems throughout the earth. Like Israel, we are to carry the cloud of His presence to a lost world and begin to fulfill our End-Time mandate.

Friendship with God

The Holy Spirit, through numerous visions, dreams and revelations, has continued to emphasize this important issue on His heart, involving intimate relationship and friendship with Him. He also highlights the strongholds and dominions that are preventing us from this all-important high calling. When these spiritual fortresses are identified, there is always a corresponding release of grace to address the issues of His heart when embraced through faith and obedience.

A number of the visions have expressed in a variety of forms our need to be spiritually balanced and in harmony with the desires and purposes of the Father. The last words our Lord spoke before His sufferings began states:

> . . . and I have made Your name known to them, and
> will make it known, so that the love with which You
> loved Me may be in them, and I in them.
>
> —JOHN 17:26

This great High Priestly prayer will be answered in its
fullness: *to love the Lord with the love of the Father*. If we
are to love the Lord with the love wherewith the Father
loved Him, we must allow the Holy Spirit to achieve in us
all that is required to live in such a blessed place.

We can love the Lord with the same love the Father had
for Him only when the Holy Spirit takes up residence in us in
His fullness. That empowering presence then catapults us
beyond the realm of human reasoning and emotions and
thrusts us into the Spirit life, imparting the divine attributes of
the Father and His redemptive names revealed to us in Jesus.

The Scriptures make it plain: Light and darkness cannot
coexist. We cannot continue to embrace worldly conformity
and expect His Holy Spirit to rest in us with His abiding
presence. His grace is being extended to enable us to be free
from the strongholds and dominions of the enemy as we
yield to this all-important work of refinement.

Coming to His people

The Church is not yet ready for the promised visitation of
the Lord as He comes to His people. In His grace, a continued
span of preparation is being allowed. Certainly, one of the key
messages for this season is the mandate concerning the soul of
man: allowing the Lord to deal with the thrones and dominions within us that remain subject to the authority of our carnal nature and worldly conformity. These seeds of corruption
were imparted into the soul of man at the Fall in the Garden
of Eden.

The incredible promise for the restoration of all things includes the blessed hope and assurance that our soul can be restored to purity and total submission to the Father. The power of redemption is more than sufficient to overcome corruption and defilement in the life of man and allows the intimate relationship with the Lord that Adam once enjoyed before the introduction of sin. One of the greatest prophetic promises for the End-Time generation is being imparted to the hearts of a hungry people desiring intimacy and union with the Lord Jesus.

The spotlight of the Holy Spirit is presently highlighting areas that have not yet been subjected to His Lordship. His Light is searching and exposing those issues resident in us that are not in conformity with God. It is sometimes a difficult and painful experience. Even so, it is of great value when we comprehend the lofty design of heaven in preparing a people for His possession. Being armed with this understanding allows the release of peace and strength needed for the battle.

Once we attain that sacred place, the powerfully anointed ministry we all desire arises on its own, like Peter. He merely walked the streets of Jerusalem, and the people positioned themselves that the glory emanating from him might touch them, providing transforming life. In such a place, we do not have to pursue ministry; rather, we will convey life every place we go. We will be the light that will shine in the midst of dark places through His abiding presence.

PART I

THE RESTORATION OF ALL THINGS

Chapter 1

IN THE BEGINNING

IN THE BEGINNING all things were obedient to God and existed in perfect harmony with His governmental design. Through the prophetic promise for the restoration of all things, we can set our faces like flint to see this design established once again. This will be true both in the Church and within us as individuals that we may know the purity originally imparted to Adam when God breathed into him the breath of life.

In this state of innocence, Adam was allowed to walk with God without veils of separation. There flourished in the Garden perfect fellowship as Adam was allowed to gaze directly into the face of God without reservation or shame. He was not overwhelmed by the purity of God. This gives us a portrayal of the original design for man and the one to which we must return.

There existed within Adam the combination of both heavenly and earthly material. Within him dwelt the divine nature and character of God veiled behind a body made from the dust of the earth.

It was God's original intent through Adam for man to live on two levels: the natural arena and the spiritual dimension with God. In the latter, we have a spiritual form that communes with God, now afforded through the process of redemption in Christ. It is the "spiritual" form of man that

the Holy Spirit is emphasizing to bring us to the place of oneness with Him, restoring what once was lost. All of creation
is groaning for this reality.

It is the determination of the Holy Spirit to compel a
company of people who will allow their spirit, soul and body
to be fully sanctified and restored to the position of fellowship and communion once enjoyed in the Garden of Eden.

As John G. Lake once said, "Real Christianity is in being
a possessor of the nature of Jesus Christ" (triune salvation).[1]
In other words, it is in being Christ in character, Christ in
demonstration, Christ in agency and in transmission.

Initial salvation

We begin to know the experience of salvation when we
surrender our spirit to the Lord and the cleansing power of
His blood. That is when we receive a conscious awareness
that our sins are forgiven and that our citizenship is now in
heaven. Our spirit has been purged by the power of His
redemption, and the Holy Spirit bears witness with our spirit
that we are redeemed. However, that is only the beginning
of the journey. Far too often many Christians fail to recognize the far-reaching implications of our redemption and its
application to our soul and our physical body.

Much has been written about the differing viewpoints
and positions of theologians involving the soul of man.
However, for the purposes of this book we will embrace the
teaching that the soul constitutes the mind, will and emotions of man. It is considered to be the seat of man's feelings,
desires, aversions and affections.

Careful biblical study of the terms *spirit* and *soul* will
clearly indicate a distinction between the two. A number of
different terminologies were used by the apostle Paul in his
epistles when teaching on the two individual aspects of our
lives. It is within the spirit that the seed of life rests until it

is quickened and made alive by the Spirit of God bringing us into an awareness of Him and our spiritual life. The author of the Book of Job seemed to understand this reality.

> But there is a spirit in man, and the breath of the Almighty gives him understanding.
>
> —JOB 32:8 (NKJV)

The soul is the seat of our personality and desires, and it must likewise be transformed from an earthly to a heavenly focus. The perfect example provided by the Lord Jesus demonstrates a fully yielded life in every aspect of His existence. He freely surrendered His thoughts and desires to assume the Father's. To be the Lord's representation on the earth, we must do likewise.

The mature sons and daughters of God will allow the Holy Spirit to fully manifest the power of redemption within their soul and restore them to the place of purity originally inherent in Adam and demonstrated in the life of the Lord Jesus Christ, our last Adam. He was a vessel fully yielded to the will of the Father.

There is an experience beyond the redemption of our spirit and even the indwelling of the Spirit with His gifts and callings: It is the yielding of our will to the will of the Father that restores us back to the fashion of His original intent.

The period of restoration

Peter, prophesying following the day of Pentecost, foretold a great redemptive promise that some generation would come to know in its fullness and reality. He emphatically declared that heaven must retain the Lord Jesus until the period of restoration of all things. The Holy Spirit, speaking through this apostle, is not simply describing the restoration of God's chosen people to a place of prominence and power.

> . . . that He may send Jesus, the Christ appointed for you, whom heaven must receive until the period of restoration of all things about which God spoke by the mouth of His holy prophets from ancient time.
>
> —Acts 3:20–21

More importantly, He is announcing the awesome power of redemption being so great and complete that a generation of God's people will come to know and experience the intimate fellowship with God formerly lost by Adam in the Garden of Eden. In fact, heaven must retain Him until there is a remnant of people who walk with that quality of companionship and oneness with God.

Wisdom, knowledge and understanding concerning all of creation were readily available to Adam through his close encounters with God as they walked in the garden. There is coming shortly a time when Christians will need to know the deep mysteries of the kingdom that ultimately will prepare her without spot or wrinkle for the Bridegroom. It will be through the decisive restoration of spiritual relationship that heavenly wisdom shall be imparted to the Bride, allowing us to "taste the good word of God and the powers of the age to come" (Hebrews 6:5).

As the Lord begins to exemplify His governmental rule and authority, it will produce the justice of God. His justice provides blessings for those who walk with Him in personal relationship and renders judgment on unrighteousness. At that time the Lord will demonstrate His favor and honor upon those who walk intimately with Him. Likewise, it will be the time of retribution and vengeance upon those who do not know Him and declined their opportunity for gospel truth.

According to the admonition given by the Holy Spirit through the apostle Paul, such people will pay the penalty and suffer the punishment of everlasting ruin and eternal separation from God. (See 2 Thessalonians 1:9.)

The restoration promises are for those who have embraced the redemption of the Lord Jesus through His sacrificial offering and resurrection power. To reject His redemption is eternal separation from the presence of the Lord and from the glory of His power.

Deep within the hearts of many Christians is the burning desire to enter that place of harmony, even if the cost is great. It is our hope that the Holy Spirit will utilize these important truths that will help us to that end.

It is not simply a matter of ministry; it is an issue of relationship *with* ministry as an overflow of the friendship we have with the Lord. After all, though we are able to heal the sick and cast out evil spirits, if the people are unable to see the Lord in us and His abiding love through us, what lasting fruit does it generate? It is not merely having the Spirit move through us but resting *in* us in His fullness.

The Lord is determined in this generation to have a people who truly *know Him* and share in His divine nature and holy character, having escaped the corruption of this world and its lusts. (See 2 Peter 1:4.) According to His grace, we are living in a season of continued refinement and purification as the Holy Spirit appraises us as individuals first before He releases the anointing of power corporately.

There is coming a time when He is going to pour out His Spirit, and it will be as rain falling on the just and the unjust alike. At that time, according to Matthew 7:21–23, there will be some doing the work of ministry whose destiny is not the kingdom of heaven but outer darkness. God forbid that any should be us. Let us walk in that place of priceless communion.

Doing the will of the Father

Matthew 7 contains one of the most dismal and unsettling

passages in all of Scripture. In it, we are told of many who will know great power performing mighty exploits in the name of the Lord. They will prophesy in the Lord's name. They will heal the sick, cast out demons and do tremendous miracles. Still, the Lord will declare to them, "I never knew you; depart from Me, you who practice lawlessness!" These are perhaps the saddest words in Scripture.

> Not everyone who says to Me, "Lord, Lord," will enter the kingdom of Heaven, but he who does the will of My Father who is in Heaven will enter. Many will say to Me on that day, "Lord, Lord, did we not prophesy in Your name, and in Your name cast out demons, and in Your name perform many miracles?" And then I will declare to them, "I never knew you; *Depart from Me, you who practice lawlessness.*"
> —MATTHEW 7:22–23 (EMPHASIS ADDED)

This passage clearly dictates that, although a person can have an anointing for ministry, he can do so without even knowing the Lord or tasting His salvation. Therefore, what is the most important matter on which we must keep ourselves focused in this hour? To know Him and the power of His resurrection—even if it means the fellowship of His sufferings. We must be conformed to His death as described in Philippians 3:10.

The highest object of endeavor in the mind of the Christian should yearn to be fully acquainted with Him and His nature, character and desires as we learn to love what He loves and hate what He hates. This will allow Him to live out His life through us as we walk in union with the Lord Jesus.

Chapter 2

WAITING ON THE LORD

WITHOUT CONTROVERSY, PART of our Great Commission is the harvest of souls and the demonstration of the Spirit and His power in our generation. There is the ministry of salvation and deliverance to set the captives free and liberate prisoners from spiritual dungeons. There is also the ministry of healing that must be carried to the people to restore the eyes of the blind, unstop deaf ears and heal lame limbs. These are all great and lofty purposes for which we devote ourselves in preparation and equipping.

Nevertheless, in the process of pursuing the Holy Spirit's power and anointing, we also discover an even higher purpose for which we are created. It is to have intimate relationship and communion with Him. Far too often we have ascertained throughout history many devoted saints who gave themselves to the work of the ministry but somehow lost the intimacy and communion that brought them to that place of anointing and power.

Consequently, we must invest ourselves to find the place of intimate exchange and sacred fellowship with the Lord and be completely unwilling to compromise that relationship for any purpose. Notice the heart's cry of the apostle Paul. Even after many years of powerful ministry, his passionate desire was to "know Him, and the power of His resurrection and the fellowship of His sufferings" (Philippians 3:10).

Mary and Martha

Through Mary and Martha the Scriptures provide a compelling example of those who earnestly desire, more than life itself, the opportunity to be joined with the Lord and find rest for their soul. This we can do when we discover the art of "waiting" upon the Lord and ministering to Him.

> But those who wait on the LORD shall renew their strength; they shall mount up with wings like eagles, they shall run and not be weary, they shall walk and not faint.
>
> —ISAIAH 40:31 (NKJV)

The two roles portrayed by the Lord's friends, Mary and Martha, illustrate a great truth for which we are compelled to pay careful attention.

The term *wait* can have dual application. One meaning is "to wait upon someone in service; to attend." Nevertheless, as utilized in this passage it means, "to tarry, to look for, to hope with expectancy; to bind together; to remain stationary in readiness or expectation; to look eagerly for someone."

The *International Standard Encyclopedia* defines it accordingly: "It implies the listening ear, a heart responsive to the wooing of God . . . a concentration of the spiritual faculties upon heavenly things . . . the patience of faith . . . the earnest expectation of the creation." (See Romans 8:19.) It describes an eager anticipation and yearning for the revelation of truth and love as it is inherent in the Father.

The adoration of Mary

Mary chose the higher call and received her strength from the Lord as she admiringly waited at His feet to receive precious enlightenment. Perhaps it was at His feet that Mary received the revelation of the Lord's approaching sacrifice and beautifully illustrated her love by anointing Him with *nard*, symbolically preparing Him for this great purpose.

Mary therefore took a pound of very costly perfume of pure nard, and anointed the feet of Jesus, and wiped His feet with her hair; and the house was filled with the fragrance of the perfume.

—JOHN 12:3

She humbly presented herself at the Lord's feet, receiving from Him the spiritual insight to anoint Him for His burial, an act few others recognized or comprehended. With only a little imagination we can visualize what it must have been like to present oneself at the Lord's feet and humbly anoint them with costly perfume. What an incredible demonstration of commitment and adoration.

Thankfully, we can, in our generation, present ourselves at His feet and give expression to our devotion through the "perfume" of commitment and worship conveyed by sanctified hearts.

This gesture of love and demonstration of spiritual vision will reveal the hearts of many as it did through Mary. The keeper of the money among the Lord's disciples responded indignantly at her beautiful presentation of love and self-sacrifice. The religious spirit in this disciple rejected this form of worship and expressed his disgust through a veiled attempt to hide his true character. Such obedience and perception of the Word will always discern and judge the thoughts and intents of people's hearts. (See Hebrews 4:12.)

There is always a time and season for each purpose characterized through Mary and Martha. There is a season to rest and wait upon the Lord and receive sufficient guidance directing our efforts toward the will of the Father and not our own inclinations. Many are presently in such a process.

It is recorded in the Scriptures: He did nothing except what He saw the Father doing and spoke only truth He heard proceed from the mouth of the Father. Likewise, we should also receive our instruction *at the Lord's feet*. As Mary sat at the Lord's feet admiringly embracing enriching truth, so also did the Lord sit at the Father's feet, receiving His counsel.

If we faithfully follow the example of Mary in this season of the Spirit, we will also receive counsel from the Lord to accomplish the will of the Father. The Lord desires to change our mind-set from that of Martha to Mary so we no longer labor *for* Him but begin to work *with* Him.

Uniquely, very often those following the example of Martha will seemingly persecute those sitting at the Lord's feet waiting on Him. It is very difficult to overcome the tendency to continually be busy about religious activity despite good intentions. It is a vitally important spiritual reality we must experience by waiting upon the Lord during the appointed seasons. It is in this place that intimacy is developed and clear comprehension of the Lord's heart.

Discovering freedom

When we recline at the Lord's feet and wait longingly for Him, we also discover freedom from our worldly conformity as we yield our will to the will of the Father. At this place of surrender we discern the thoughts and desires of the Lord, displacing our own. Our thoughts are not His thoughts, and our earthly ways are foreign to His. Yet, at His feet we can ascertain the path of righteousness and spiritual conformity according to the council of the Holy Spirit.

Along with Mary, we discover in the Gospels another precious woman who lovingly washed the Lord's feet with her tears and dried them with her hair in a sacrificial gesture of respect and love. She clearly disregarded the reproach of men in order to fulfill this great demonstration of discernment and affection. The Church must come to the same place.

> **And behold, there was a woman in the city who was a sinner; and when she learned that He was reclining at the table in the Pharisee's house, she brought an alabaster vial of perfume, and standing behind Him at His feet, weeping, she began to wet His feet with her tears, and kept wiping them with the hair of her head, and kissing His feet, and anointing them with the perfume.**
>
> **—LUKE 7:37–38**

Many times in prophetic experiences, a person's hair is representative of their glory or of their intellect. We lay our thoughts and opinions (intellect) at the Lord's feet and begin to take upon ourselves "the mind of Christ" through the impartation of the Holy Spirit. This woman fulfilled the responsibility of the law by doing honor to this most acclaimed of guests, although the Pharisees had failed to meet their legal obligations of washing and honoring a distinguished visitor.

She retrieved an alabaster box containing all she had achieved in her sinful and worldly pursuits. She unsparingly lavished this substance of great value upon the Lord, disregarding the cost. Previously, she had lived in darkness and pursued the desires of her heart through unjust gain. However, now that Light had come into the world, she emerged from her dark stupor and repented by abandoning all self-regard and fear of man to disperse upon the Lord her resources.

This dear sister who washed the Lord's feet and dried them with her hair had previously placed her security in the

spirit of this world. Upon recognizing the divine Light that
had entered the realm of man, she rejected the security
offered by the spirit of this world and whole-heartedly dis-
pensed herself upon the Lord in an expression of affection
and trust. She found rest for her soul in Him and abandoned
all else to give expression to her new-found life.

It is at His feet that we lay all of our ability and essence,
humbly acknowledging our great need for Him and His
resources. It is at His feet that we begin to bridge the gap
between the vast and infinite provision of heaven and the
great need of humanity.

Traditions of man

Although this woman was recognized as an adulteress,
reality highlighted that the Pharisees were guilty of a greater
sin in their spiritual adultery, although they were busily fulfilling the traditions of the law. Their sin blinded them to the
spiritual gift directly before them and nullified the grace of
God extended to them.

They were so preoccupied in religious duty that they neg-
lected to receive the revelation of God. Because of this neg-
ligence they forfeited their ability to properly lead and
prepare the people for their divine visitation. They were
absorbed in dutifully complying with the precepts of man
and following human traditions, and they were blinded to
the very presence of God in their midst.

Additionally, the other religious leaders in the room
expressed their disgust and dismay at their perceived notion
that the Lord lacked the discernment to detect this woman's
previous character. The Lord responded to these leaders by
essentially disclosing that their names would not be remembered a few years from that point, yet this woman's testimony
would be remembered for all generations.

The Lord chastised the Pharisees for not recognizing

their great responsibility. It was their duty to be the leaders of Israel and discern the Light that had come into their dark world. Regardless, because of their hardness of heart they were unable to ascertain the day of their visitation or to prepare the people of their generation for the Lord's purpose.

Their pure example

Few leaders of His day were willing to sit at the Lord's feet to receive instruction. Only those with humbleness of heart, like these two women, could receive that edification. The example of these two women is an eternal illustration for all who are willing to do likewise.

There is a time for waiting and a time for executing. However, the performing of religious or spiritual endeavors is after we have waited upon the Lord to receive divine instruction and counsel and begin to bear His image.

Likewise, Martha, although doing something that seemed appropriate, failed to recognize the greater purpose of sitting at the Lord's feet absorbing every available impartation. There is a time to wait and a time to do. We must ask the Lord for the discernment to distinguish the two and take full advantage of the times of preparation and refinement.

By no means is this prophetic analogy intended to endorse slothfulness. Instead, it is designed to encourage the Church to first receive instruction at the Lord's feet by waiting upon Him, then employing the gifts and means available in the accomplishment of these divine purposes. It is in ministering to Him that we distinguish His thoughts and ways.

Chapter 3

PREPARED BY THE ANOINTING FOR OUR DESTINY

PRESENTLY MUCH OF the Church is in a posture of waiting upon the Lord during this season to receive from Him divine instruction for the upcoming outpouring of the Spirit. There presently seems to be significant importance placed upon the role of sitting at the Lord's feet to receive the will of the Father.

> Not everyone who says to Me, "Lord, Lord," will enter the kingdom of heaven, but he who does the will of My Father in heaven.
>
> —MATTHEW 7:21 (NKJV)

There is approaching a time in which we will be very busy about the Lord's business. If we will follow this standard of waiting upon the Lord and ministering to Him, it will allow Him to restore us to a place of innocence. Then our efforts will be far more profitable and achieve much more with considerably less extended effort.

Appreciable gain will be achieved in the realm of the Spirit when operating under the spirit of wisdom and understanding. When we receive the wisdom of heaven and the

understanding of that revelation, we unlock divine principles essential for accomplishing the will of the Father. Very
often we recognize an end to be achieved, but we go about
it with our own understanding, consuming greater energy
and time to complete the assignment.

Waiting upon the Lord has virtually been a lost art in the
corporate Church. It is imperative that we begin to appre-
hend this great spiritual principle in accomplishing the divine
purposes established for this period of Church history. The
Lord is far more interested in our obedience than our human
efforts. He is much more concerned with the development of
our spiritual discernment than our human zeal.

Resting in Him

In our call to minister the gospel to a lost world, we are
often set apart and charged with a specific calling on behalf
of the kingdom of heaven. However, it can sometimes be
months or even years before the commission or authority is
released in the realization of those purposes.

During the interim, we should follow the example of Paul
who discovered the Lord's rest and separated himself unto
the Lord. It was in a place of separation that he allowed the
Holy Spirit to prepare him for the great purposes ahead.

Paul was called as an apostle to the Gentiles, but he was
not equipped and commissioned for that purpose until many
years later. The time he spent faithfully waiting upon the
Lord qualified him to do the will of the Father in his life.

It was many years later at Antioch that the Holy Spirit
instructed the leaders to set apart Barnabas and Saul for the
apostolic work for which they had been created. They were
among the prophets and teachers, but the time had come
for their high calling and ultimate mandate. The anointing
in them had provided the equipping and refining necessary
to be promoted to the apostolic office.

Just as He teaches you

The Bible teaches that, when we become Christians, we receive an anointing from God. It is through the impartation of His anointing that we learn to dwell in Him and walk in the ministry of the Spirit.

> And as for you, the anointing which you received from Him abides in you, and you have no need for anyone to teach you; but as His anointing teaches you about all things, and is true and is not a lie, and just as it has taught you, you abide in Him.
>
> —1 John 2:27

There has been an ancient question existing among men for many centuries. Why am I here, and for what purpose have I been created? The answer can be discovered through the anointing of the Holy Spirit resident in us. We can also ascertain our calling and purpose within the body of Christ and the divine destiny appointed for us. That is our promise from this passage.

According to this scripture, the anointing will teach us all that we need to know to fulfill our God-ordained destiny in life. When a true prophetic word has been spoken to an individual concerning his or her calling and future, an impartation of the anointing is released to equip him or her to fulfill that purpose. The Lord will perfectly mold and fashion us to accomplish His directive through the anointing we receive.

Far too often, we do not allow His anointing to prepare and direct us to the place of our fruitfulness in Him. Oftentimes, we observe a certain ministry or minister that we recognize is being used by the Lord, and we try to emulate them or mold ourselves into the framework of that ministry. However, that may not be the purpose for which we have been created, nor the direction for which the anointing within us is trying to orchestrate.

Likewise, many educational institutions attempt to develop leaders into a certain image through theological indoctrination and other patterns and formulas. However, this scripture points out that His anointing teaches us about all things. Just as He teaches us, so shall we abide in Him.

This is not to say we do not follow the anointed teaching and instructions given through men. Rather, it dictates that the Holy Spirit will lead us to the specific teachings and teachers that He recognizes will prepare us for our destiny. The Lord has established His leadership and government to equip the body to do the work of the ministry. This is accomplished in a variety of ways . . . but always by His leading.

We are living in the days identified as the *time of the end.* There is a specific and unique destiny placed upon this generation. Many prophets of old foresaw this day and the great purposes of heaven to be attained. Many patriarchs yearned for this day and were not allowed to experience the unfolding of God's "grand finale." We, on our watch, will have the privilege to see and encounter incredible things.

There is a specific anointing being released from heaven with a corresponding grace to teach us how to abide in Him for the unique mandate to our generation. Only by the Holy Spirit, through the anointing resident in us, can we be adequately prepared for the unprecedented demands shortly to unfold.

The preparation of Paul

The Lord met Saul on the road to Damascus and set him on the path to achieve the high calling and apostolic destiny placed upon his life. The Lord sent one of His closest friends to the newly converted Saul to confer a prophetic word and calling that would direct the remainder of Paul's life.

And it came about that as he journeyed, he was approaching Damascus, and suddenly a light from heaven flashed around him; and he fell to the ground, and heard a voice saying to him, "Saul, Saul, why are you persecuting Me?" And he said, "Who art Thou, Lord?" And He said, "I am Jesus whom you are persecuting . . . "

—Acts 9:3

Now there was a certain disciple at Damascus, named Ananias; and the Lord said to him in a vision, "Ananias." And he said, "Behold, here am I, Lord." And the Lord said to him, "Arise and go to the street called Straight, and inquire at the house of Judas for a man from Tarsus named Saul, for behold, he is praying."

—Acts 9:10–11

It is an interesting correlation to observe the two replies given by Saul and by Ananias in response to the open visions given to each. You can hear the distress in the voice of Saul as he exclaimed, "Who art thou, Lord?" Also notice the affection and devotion in the words of Ananias, "Behold, here am I, Lord."

Ananias had clearly encountered the Lord in previous spiritual experiences and developed an open relationship and communion with Him. This devoted saint was being given the great privilege of pronouncing the calling and commission placed upon the life of Paul and setting him on the course of his apostolic destiny.

The Lord instructed His consecrated friend, Ananias, to lay hands on Saul and prophesy that he would know the will of God, see the Righteous One, and hear utterances from His lips. Perhaps Ananias did not initially recognize this as a distinguished privilege. He responded to the Lord that he had heard about Saul and the threats and oppressions he carried against those in the Christian way. As if that instruction was not difficult enough, he was also told that he must disclose to Saul all he would suffer for the sake of the gospel. What a difficult task this must have been for the obedience of Ananias. Yet this loyal and devoted saint fully accomplished the task given to him.

Cooperating with the anointing

Following the tremendous encounter and release of destiny, the anointing that accompanied the prophetic directive began to teach Paul how to abide in the Lord and become an apostolic leader and pillar of the Church. So shall it be with us.

The anointing resident in us will prepare us for our place in the mystical body of Christ and point us to our high calling. It will be the place of our authority and fruitfulness. We must cooperate with the Holy Spirit and fully yield to His anointing. We are colaborers with Him in the submission of our soul to His agenda. When we cooperate with God we become "co-operators" of His provision and purpose, and we should never allow ourselves to remove Him from the integral place of leadership.

Without controversy, the anointing that is resident within many Christians is presently inviting and beckoning them to a place of intimate relationship and close communion not unlike the friendship expressed between the Lord and Ananias. Little is written about this notable saint after his encounter with Paul. One thing is certain: He may not have been widely known among men, but he was certainly well known in heaven.

Ananias' account illustrates that we do not necessarily have to be called as a prominent apostle or prophet with a large ministry and following to have an intimate, face-to-face relationship with the Lord and carry great spiritual authority.

Some historical documentation suggests Ananias later became a deacon in the church at Damascus. Otherwise, little else is recorded.

Our greatest attribute is to possess desire, an unwavering and undeniable yearning and hunger to be a faithful friend to the Lord Jesus and a trustworthy steward of the mysteries and power of God, to stand before Him face-to-face and speak with Him as a friend speaks to his friend. Our sincere petition is to be endowed with a pure heart and right motives and clothed with a spirit of humility that we may know Him as fully as He may be known—a desire to be like Him that He may rest in us.

Awakening to destiny

One of the great mysteries to be fully realized during the End-Time generation is that of Christ in us, the hope of glory. Christ, the anointing and anointed One, resident in us, provides a revolutionizing power and divine vitalization that transforms and awakens us to our destiny. The Lord Jesus has a purpose and design for each individual to reveal Himself in and through us.

The high purpose of heaven is to bring all of the elements of our being and existence into harmony with Him and His will for our lives. This is true not only within our spirits but also our mind, will and emotions, that we may fully possess the mind of Christ for us. This is primarily true in our relationship with Him and also the ministry we are to carry to this generation.

God is not looking for men and women to make replicas or clones of themselves. He is desiring to fully possess the spirit, soul and body of His people and utilize their individuality and godly qualities inherent in them.

The Scriptures point out that we were in Christ before the foundation of the world. It is His desire to express the qualities He has placed in each of us as individuals who will fully constitute His body. The Lord is not looking to destroy our individuality, only the seeds of corruption that keep us from becoming the full expression of His qualities and attributes and the uniqueness for which we have been created.

When a company of people is allowed to enter complete union with Christ, it will provide the place in which heaven touches earth. It will be the true Bethel and house of God—the place in which angels ascend and descend.

The heavenly Father is going to unleash great spiritual authority with divine revelation as the hearts of men come into agreement with the purposes of God. This merger, or union, between heaven and earth will produce the great miracles, signs and wonders prophesied for this generation. When we agree with God, we are, in actuality, agreeing to love.

Through compassion and bearing His divine attributes, we will unleash the great resources of heaven for the vast need of humanity. The miracles, signs and wonders are not the end in themselves but the by-product of the expression of divine love through His people. Healing is always birthed through compassion.

This defines the high calling for our generation. A great grace is being allotted to help us achieve this place of consecration and purity. It will provide the cleansing of the earthly nature resident in us by the indwelling power of the Holy Spirit. It will facilitate the transforming of our mind and nature into conformity with the mind and nature of the Lord Jesus.

Clearly, there is resident in the hearts of many sincere Christians a yearning desire to live free from the spirit of this world and the compulsions of its lusts. However, to truly accommodate that purpose we must have resident in us His empowering presence and the fullness of the Spirit, which changes our spiritual DNA and internal makeup. The Spirit dwelling in us is compelling us to a higher place in Him.

PART II

THRONES OF OUR SOUL

Chapter 4

PARTAKERS OF HIS NATURE— THE VISION

THE ADMONITION OF the Holy Spirit through the apostle Paul charges us to be *fully* sanctified in every department of life. We are triune beings, and our salvation must inherently be applied accordingly.

To be delivered from our natural inclinations, thoughts and ways, we must yield ourselves to the refining work of the Holy Spirit within our soul or mind to possess the mind of Christ. From this place of surrender, we embark on the spiritual journey to reflect the image of Christ and portray His attributes and power.

This place of sanctification is the prophetic fulfillment of 2 Peter 1:4, making us partakers of the divine nature and escaping the corruption of this world and its lusts.

> Seeing that His divine power has granted to us everything pertaining to life and godliness, through the true knowledge of Him who called us by His own glory and excellence. For by these He has granted to us His precious and magnificent promises, in order that by them you might become partakers of the

divine nature, having escaped the corruption that is
in the world by lust.

—2 Peter 1:3–4

This reality was portrayed in a prophetic experience that
has left a significant impact upon me and a hunger to see it
fulfilled in our generation . . . by the grace of God.

The experience

During the early part of 1999, my wife, Wanda, and I
entered a season of prayer and intercession concerning the
upcoming year and the teachings we were to deliver to
God's people as fresh manna. While entreating the Lord in
this manner, a new arena of prophetic teachings was
"downloaded" to help us enter the place of habitation and
intimacy we passionately desire. Some of the revelations
were given through prophetic experiences, which highlighted convincing portions of Scripture that are essential in
this quest.

The following is an allegorical experience graciously
allowed to convey important principles essential for our
development and training for the soon-coming spiritual
releases from heaven. In it, much prophetic symbolism is
utilized to communicate prominent spiritual truths to help
us advance to maturity and a deep place of intimacy with
the Lord.

Many layers of understanding can be derived from revelations of this nature. I hope to accurately share the vision
and its scriptural and historical foundation, and ask the
Holy Spirit to lead each reader to greater depths of understanding unique to their specific circumstances and level of
maturity.

Eighteen thrones

In this experience, an angel standing to my right took me

into the realm of the Spirit. Initially, this measureless and far-reaching domain appeared vast and dark, in much the same manner we would expect empty space to appear. However, far above I could see a glimmering light to which we traveled in an instant of time.

In this place I could see easily a circle, or ring, of thrones, approximately eighteen in number and forming a perfect sphere. These seats of authority did not have the appearance we would normally associate with thrones established on the earth. Instead, they appeared to be oval-shaped orbs of light.

I was taken to a place adjacent to the first throne and discovered that an angel of the Lord occupied it. The angel inhabited the throne with authority and dominion, standing majestically as a soldier would guard his post of duty.

I was taken to the next throne, which was inhabited by an angel of the Lord like the first. However, when I was taken to the next throne, a most disappointing and disturbing sight loomed. Instead of the angel of the Lord, the throne was occupied by a hideous creature usurping a position rightfully belonging to the Lord. It is difficult to fashion words to describe the grotesque, perverted appearance of the evil being. It is sufficient to say that he was the opposite of everything pure and godly.

Upon making this discovery, the angel standing to my right handed me an implement filled with water. I instinctively knew I was to begin pouring water on the creature. The moment I did, the evil spirit lashed at me with his paw as a lion would strike its prey.

Startled, I looked at my chest, expecting it to be torn to shreds. Instead, I was uninjured by the assault. Encouraged, I began to pour the water freely until the creature began to diminish and eventually vanish from the throne. When this occurred, the angel of the Lord emerged, taking his residence on the throne.

As I contemplated the remaining thrones, I noticed that many were occupied by an angel of the Lord, and many by repulsive creatures. In each case where the throne was occupied by one of these beasts, I would simply begin pouring water on the spirit until it disappeared from the throne and an angel of the Lord appeared.

The soul of man

I was later instructed that the ring of thrones constituted the soul of man. The term *throne* is defined as "the seat occupied by a ruler or high official." It is considered to be the office, rank or authority of a ruler or one having dominion and authority within a jurisdiction.

In this symbolic revelation, each throne represented a department of our individual lives that constitutes our mind, will and emotions. From these dominions within us, our actions, expressions and meditations are governed. According to the original design of heaven, each throne was intended to be subjected to the lordship of Christ. However, because of the curse of the fallen nature, some of the thrones are given over to the spirit of the world.

> And do not be conformed to this world, but be transformed by the renewing of your mind, that you may prove what the will of God is, that which is good and acceptable and perfect.
>
> —ROMANS 12:2

In all of those areas where we had totally submitted ourselves to the dominion and rulership of God, the angel of the Lord occupied the throne. Likewise, in each realm where we had not fully yielded ourselves, the carnal nature ruled and had authority. The unholy administration was represented by the creature that was given opportunity to occupy the throne. He usurped a position rightfully belonging to God.

Through the redemptive process and the impartation of grace, these thrones are sanctified and brought under the Lord's rulership. For complete union with Christ, each throne must be occupied by the Lord. Unfortunately, we oftentimes allow the spirit of the world to inhabit the thrones within our soul, placing a veil over our "face" that prohibits complete fellowship with God.

> Now the deeds of the flesh are evident, which are: immorality, impurity, sensuality, idolatry, sorcery, enmities, strife, jealousy, outbursts of anger, disputes, dissensions, factions, envying, drunkenness, carousing, and things like these, of which I forewarn you just as I have forewarned you that those who practice such things shall not inherit the kingdom of God.
>
> —GALATIANS 5:19–21

The Scriptures report that the veil of the Temple was rent from top to bottom through the sacrificial offering of the Lord's body. Therefore, if we are not seeing the Lord clearly, it is because the veils remain over *our* soul. It is through the "water of the Word" that the issues of our soul are exposed and sanctified.

> For thou wilt light my candle: the LORD my God will enlighten my darkness.
>
> —PSALM 18:28 (KJV)

All things are open and laid bare before the eyes of the Living Word. There is not a creature that exists who can conceal himself from the penetrating view of the Lord. As the Scriptures plainly point out, He is alive, full of power, and sharper than a two-edged sword—exposing, analyzing and judging the very thoughts and purposes of man's heart.

For the word of God is living and active and sharper than any two-edged sword, and piercing as far as the division of soul and spirit, of both joints and marrow, and able to judge the thoughts and intentions of the heart.

—HEBREWS 4:12

Chapter 5

WASHED BY THE WORD

IT IS PRESENTLY the desire of the Holy Spirit to create radical purity essential for our entering the secret place of the Most High and union with Christ. The emphasis of the Spirit is now fixed on the cleansing and purifying work necessary for believers to enter a higher dimension of anointing and relationship.

> . . . that He might sanctify her, having cleansed her by the washing of water with the word, that He might present to Himself the church in all her glory, having no spot or wrinkle or any such thing; but that she should be holy and blameless.
>
> —EPHESIANS 5:26–27

When the anointing of the Holy Spirit quickens the Word with life and power, it allows truth to penetrate into the very fiber of our being, transforming us into the likeness of Christ. When the ultimate process of sanctification has been achieved, it will present us to the bridegroom in the fullness of His reflection: That is being washed by the water of the Word.

The Holy Spirit will identify issues within us contrary to His nature and quicken the Word of Truth to provide a divine alternative. When we embrace the revealed Truth with our arms of faith, it will begin to change our nature and character, creating purity and a Christlike mind.

The mark of genuine Christianity is clearly recognized in the virtue of a consecrated life. This takes place when our thoughts and ways are made to be consistent with His. It is in the possession of the mind of Christ that we discover the secrets of His kingdom and embrace the keys that unlock the vast resources of our promised inheritance.

> Be anxious for nothing, but in everything by prayer and supplication with thanksgiving let your requests be made known to God. And the peace of God, which surpasses all comprehension, shall *guard your hearts and your minds in Christ Jesus.*
> —PHILIPPIANS 4:6–7 (EMPHASIS ADDED)

There is available in God a place of peace and rest that serves as a guard, or garrison, over our hearts and minds. The term "guard" is taken from *phroureo,* meaning "to protect by a military guard or to prevent hostile invasion or an unwanted besieging." A spiritual watch is assigned to govern and express the pure and powerful qualities of God.

An alternative teaching

Unfortunately, there is a prevailing message being taught throughout the American Church that is rooted in the spirit of the world, preparing people to walk by an independent spirit rather than being led by the Spirit of God. Many people are being trained to deliver themselves through self-reliance and humanistic preparation. This mentality clearly grieves the Holy Spirit and actually works a counter-productivity in readying the Church for weighty milestones coming to the earth. Our preparation is a spiritual one, requiring a spiritual provision that comes from the very heart of the Father.

Many books, journals and spoken messages are being directed at maintaining a comfortable way of life instead of preparation to be clothed in robes of righteousness. Much is being distributed to teach people various means of self-preservation and provisional hoarding. However, the overcoming Church will clearly recognize that her help comes from the Lord, and His abundant provision of grace will allow her to walk closely with Him through the washing of His Word.

When Israel was delivered from the bondage of Egypt, the Lord was their source, faithfully providing for every need. He accompanied them by the pillar of fire at night and the cloud by day. He is the same—yesterday, today and forever. Our highest purpose is to return to the place of fellowship and empowering presence once lost through sin but now available through His redemption. Our role is to recognize this mandate and cooperate with the Holy Spirit who qualifies us for union.

If a person truly desires to be prepared for the twenty-first century and utilized by the Holy Spirit to meet the needs of this generation, he should be doing all the Lord would require in order to be clothed with Christ, having a righteousness that comes from God through faith. We must consider the loss of all things for the sake of gaining Christ, and we should consider the loss as mere rubbish compared to the surpassing value of union with the Lord Jesus. (See Philippians 3:8–9.)

Our treasures must be stored in heaven where neither moth nor rust can destroy, nor thieves break in and steal it.

For the mind set on the flesh is death, but the mind set on the Spirit is life and peace, because the mind set on the flesh is hostile toward God; for it does not subject itself to the law of God, for it is not even able

to do so; and those who are in the flesh cannot please God.

—ROMANS 8:6–8

Our high calling can be discovered through emptying ourselves of our own inclinations and opinions through the washing of His anointed Word and relying upon the faithful leading of the Holy Spirit. It is through the stripping process and assuming the heart of a servant that true spiritual authority is recognized in heaven. A bondservant is one who yields his will to the will of his master.

> . . . [He] emptied Himself, taking the form of a bond-servant, and being made in the likeness of men. And being found in appearance as a man, He humbled Himself by becoming obedient to the point of death, even death on a cross.
>
> —PHILIPPIANS 2:7–8

A counterfeit message

There are religious spirits roving to and fro seeking a forum to impart legalism, opinion, debate, judgment and criticism inherently appealing to the needs of the flesh. The religious spirit will produce death and hostility toward God, while the Holy Spirit generates life.

The benefits of the kingdom of heaven are His glory, lovingkindness, mercy, righteousness and peace produced through the Spirit of Truth. If we are going to be fruitful, we must be faithful to the Spirit of Truth. It should be the heart's cry of all God's people to see the glory abiding in the land.

> For Thy lovingkindness is before my eyes, and I have walked in Thy truth.
>
> —PSALM 26:3

The Spirit of Truth will expose the deceptions and counterfeit messages introduced through the religious spirit. It is
only by this spiritual impartation that true discernment is
generated.

The Lord Jesus foretold that a false spirit would be
released that would characterize the time of the end so much
like the genuine article that it would deceive the very elect if
possible.

**For false christs and false prophets will rise and show
great signs and wonders to deceive, if possible, even
the elect.**

—MATTHEW 24:24 (NKJV)

Only by the indwelling presence of the Spirit of Truth
can we discern the distinction. A careful examination of
Church history clearly identifies the power of this deception
and its intent to steal our inheritance. It will produce a form
of godliness that denies the power thereof.

When accomplished, great conflict results between the
two camps. We are confronted with making difficult
choices. The high road will require submission in every
arena of our being and a willingness to bear the reproach
that will come when wholly consecrated to Him.

If we embrace the correct commission, we will be cata-
pulted to greater measures of lovingkindness and righteousness and experience heightened expressions of His glory.

Instead of religious debate, which destroys faith and
results in an independent spirit, we will become dependent
totally upon the Lord as a yielded vessel washed in the truth
of His Word. Rather than living by a judgmental spirit of
criticism, we will sow mercy at every opportunity in order to
receive mercy. (See James 2:13.)

When we allow grace for the failures of others we will

also reap grace for our own shortcomings. Instead of criticism we will look at others through the "new wine" of grace.

The new wine

The Lord turned water into wine at the wedding of Cana, embarking on a ministry of miracles and preaching of righteousness. So shall the "wine" reserved for this generation do likewise. The Holy Spirit is releasing a prophetic mandate, announcing His desire for His servants to preach life, expectancy and preparation for visitation from the Lord and rehearsal for the wedding celebration. Instead of "strong drink," the Lord is bringing "new wine."

The covenant in "new wine" allows us to look at God and our fellow man with an entirely new perspective. The letter of the law kills, but the Spirit gives life. The religious spirit desires the yoke of the law, while the Holy Spirit is a life-giving Spirit. The Spirit of Truth will also serve as a tutor, leading us into a life of purity and holiness and guiding us to freedom from the carnal nature and liberty in Christ.

Legalism is the opposite of righteousness. Noah was a preacher of righteousness and was preserved in the day of judgment. No humanistic counsel could have prepared him for the events that unfolded. Only divine revelation equipped him for the unprecedented events that ultimately destroyed the world.

Many of the events taking place in our generation will be unprecedented circumstances requiring counsel that will come from behind the veil through the Spirit of Wisdom and revelation. We must be willing to pay the price to be cleansed and purified to be joined with Christ and taken to the throne room of God to receive our instruction and begin to comprehend the mysteries of the kingdom.

Chapter 6

THE REFINEMENT
OF ABRAHAM

THE GREAT PATRIARCH Abraham experienced the purging process of his soul for complete union with God. After the promise had been fulfilled and Isaac was born, the Scriptures clearly express that Abraham loved his son with a great love. So intense was his love for Isaac that it actually became an idol, usurping a position in Abraham that rightfully belonged to God.

Abraham was required to demonstrate the complete dedication of his soul to God by willingly submitting the life of Isaac to the Lord. Upon the successful completion of this test, Abraham was able to worship God on an elevated level that he would not have known otherwise.

Our "Isaacs" can be representative of many things we allow that separate us from our highest purpose in God. Very often, "Isaac" is symbolic of our prophetic promises or ministry that we enable to occupy a place of preeminence belonging only to God. Though the purging process is painful, it is necessary to become one spirit with Christ. It is the literal fulfillment of Galatians 2:20.

In the same way Abraham was provided an alternative so also are we being supplied with a divine alternative from the Lord our provider. The Lord Jesus has made provision for us *if* we follow His prescribed way. Those areas in us usurping a position rightfully belonging to Him can be extracted and replaced with divine attributes afforded by the power of His resurrection.

Learning from the past

Church history is filled with many honorable men and women of the past who had powerfully anointed ministries that ultimately ended in failure and humiliation. This is primarily true because there was some corruption or self-serving motive that regrettably emerged at the pinnacle of their ministry.

For the most part, these were good, godly people who began their ministry with pure motives and paid a great price in their service to God. Many of the truths we commonly walk in today are the result of their pioneering work and sacrificial labor. Several of the healing evangelists of the 1940s and 1950s spent extended times in prayer and fasting in their service to God and their quest to be anointed with power. If we could hear a message from the cloud of witnesses, I am certain they would admonish us to learn from their mistakes so we can get it right in our day.

By studying the healing revival of the twentieth century, we discover that many of the ministries ended in shipwreck and disillusionment. Unfortunately, seeds of corruption remained hidden in their souls, into which Satan was able to sink his hooks, causing great confusion and collapse. When we examine the successes and failures of our Church fathers we can derive important spiritual lessons.

One of our noble obligations is honoring God's men and women of the past as we contemplate the lives of great Church leaders. There is a man who, in my estimation, was one of the foremost of this century, Alexander Dowie.

Dowie was a powerfully anointed leader during the years preceding and following the turn of the twentieth century. He was wonderfully used of the Lord in the ministry of healing and was a prolific writer of Scriptural truth.

His periodical, "Leaves of Healing," was delivered to an international audience, introducing the power of God to the universal Church. Unfortunately, Brother Dowie is remembered more for the "Elijah proclamation" than for the awesome ways in which he was used by the Holy Spirit in his generation.

The hook

Dowie records in his journal that two men requested an audience with him to share the "word" they reportedly had received from the Lord. During the meeting, these Christian men prophesied to Brother Dowie they had received a revelation disclosing that he was the prophesied Elijah. Clearly, these men were deceived.

Alexander Dowie was so upset with their words that he immediately expelled them from his office. However, Dowie further records that their words were "like a hook embedded" in his heart. No matter how earnestly he tried, Brother Dowie was unable to free himself from the weight of this proclamation. In the years that followed, the demonically inspired lie grew within his soul until Dowie proclaimed himself "Elijah the Restorer."[1]

How could such a tragic mistake befall a precious man of God wonderfully used by the Holy Spirit? I recently posed that question to a prophetic acquaintance who shared how the Lord had specifically spoken on this very subject in a powerful prophetic experience.

In the revelation, the Lord instructed that great men of God with powerful anointing of the Spirit fall prey to the traps of the enemy because their souls are not fully purged of the carnal nature. As in Brother Dowie's case, there were issues within his soul that the Lord desired to address but was unable to extract for reasons known only to God. There were carnal thrones within him that had not been subjected to the Lord's dominion. This left opportunity for the enemy to exploit the seeds of ambition or pride, resulting in spiritual error and the collapse of his ministry.

It was the seed of corruption that was imparted into the soul of man at the fall in the Garden of Eden. Explicitly, the Bible predicts that all things will be restored. Heaven must retain the Lord until there is the restoration of all things promised through the prophets. That is, a people for His own possession with whom He can have intimate relationship and through whom He can express His divine attributes and power.

We are presently living in a time characterized by God's grace, allowing the restoration of our soul to the place where we can experience the fellowship with God that was lost in the Garden of Eden. The only thing hindering us from that relationship is ourselves. It is the dominion of the carnal nature residing in us from which we can be freed.

PART III

VESSELS OF LIFE

Chapter 7

FLOWING LIKE
A RIVER

ALL OF US enjoy the convenience of having water supplied to our homes through modern plumbing systems. The water is provided through pipes. The pipes themselves do not furnish the water but merely provide the vessel through which the water flows. As the water continually streams through the pipes, they are constantly kept clean by the circulation of water.

Likewise, we are the vessels through which the River of Life flows, and we are perpetually made clean through union with the Source of Life. As we abide in Him and He in us, the River of Life surges through us to those in need and provides a source of cleansing and refreshing from His presence.

The admonition in this hour is to so thoroughly allow the purging and purification of our soul that there would be no veils to separate us from the Lord's face. There would be neither hindrances nor restraints in the relationship we have with Him.

The triune salvation described in 1 Thessalonians 5:23 relates the full redemption of the spirit, soul and body of the believer. The mind, will and emotions of man are made complete through the Lord's great redemption, allowing us to become one Spirit with Him in perfect fellowship.

Now may the God of peace Himself sanctify you entirely; and may your spirit and soul and body be preserved complete, without blame at the coming of our Lord Jesus Christ.

—1 THESSALONIANS 5:23

Many things are allowed to occupy the thrones of our soul and will vary with every individual. However, each can be traced to the carnal nature of man and the elevation of "self." A glorious opportunity is being offered to those who are willing to pay the price and experience the purging process for the joy of perfect fellowship after its completion.

We should each pray that the Holy Spirit will reveal areas of our souls that remain subject to the carnal nature. Through repentance and the yielding of our will, He will extract worldly passions and impart the Divine Nature. We are given the magnificent opportunity to come to the Lord and take His yoke upon us . . . *and find rest for our souls.*

Strongholds and dominions

The thrones and dominions under the jurisdiction of the enemy are the result of seeds imparted through the fallen nature as the result of sin originating in the Garden of Eden. The prophet David once said:

Behold, I was brought forth in iniquity, and in sin my mother conceived me.

—PSALM 51:5

Many individuals battle strongholds of the enemy that were transferred through generational bloodlines and are imparted in birth through parents. These are sometimes called "generational curses." Though we were born with seeds of corruption, that does not mean they should be allowed to remain. It is not necessary to continue to battle the same spiritual enemies that plagued our father and his father and his father before him.

The generational curses can stop *now*. Freedom from the sins of our fathers is at hand. Simply because our father or mother battled depression, rejection or lust does not mean we must live with these same adversaries. Through repentance and prayer, grace is being released to free us from the reproach of generational afflictions so the Lord's face can shine upon us, His desolate sanctuary.

> O Lord, in accordance with all Thy righteous acts, let now Thine anger and Thy wrath turn away from Thy city Jerusalem, Thy holy mountain; for because of our sins and the iniquities of our fathers, Jerusalem and Thy people have become a reproach to all those around us. So now, our God, listen to the prayer of Thy servant and to his supplications, and for Thy sake, O Lord, let Thy face shine on Thy desolate sanctuary.
> —DANIEL 9:16–17

The time has now come for the Church to be free from the dominion of the enemy and set on the course for liberty and freedom through the Holy Spirit. We must not allow these things to separate us from God any longer. Though strongholds and dominions can alienate us from the knowledge and awareness of His manifest presence, they cannot separate us from His love.

His love is abounding and lavished toward us. So great is His love that He will not allow us to continue on a path of destruction to our own demise. It is His mercy that brings correction and releases grace to liberate us from the strongholds and dominions of the enemy.

Stronghold defined

The term "stronghold" is taken from the word *ochuroma* meaning, "a castle, stronghold, fortress, security or anything on which one relies." It is used of the arguments and reasonings by which a disputant endeavors to fortify his opinion and defend it against his opponent. *Webster's Dictionary* conveys the meaning as "a fortified place or a place dominated by a particular group marked by a particular characteristic."

From these meanings we can discern that a stronghold is a fortified place within our soul dominated by a particular characteristic that is contrary to the character and nature of God.

A dominion is likewise defined as "the ability or strength with which one is endued, which he either possesses or exercises. It is the power of authority or influence and of right and privilege, such as authority over mankind or a thing subject to authority or rule within a jurisdiction." *Webster's* records a dominion as "a domain or supreme authority and sovereignty."

Therefore a carnal dominion can be understood as a sphere of authority granted that allows the exercise of influence over one's thoughts and actions opposed to the mandates of Scripture and the representations of a righteous life.

The Lord alone is to occupy the thrones of our soul, having complete dominion and authority over the purchase of His blood. Any other power usurping that place of authority rightfully belonging to Him creates conflict within us and a veil over our soul, separating us from the fullness of His presence.

Loving the Lord with *all* our heart

If we are to fulfill the biblical mandate to love the Lord

our God with all our heart, soul and strength, we must experience the reality of yielding our will to the will of the Father and apprehending the purification and refinement in each area of our lives.

> You shall love the LORD your God with all your heart, with all your soul, and with all your strength.
> —DEUTERONOMY 6:5 (NKJV)

The foundation for this principle resides in his abundant love for us and our love and appreciation toward Him for His great work of redemption. This war is presently raging in the souls of those being prepared to be used mightily of the Spirit in our day.

> . . . I see a different law in the members of my body, waging war against the law of my mind, and making me a prisoner of the law of sin which is in my members. Wretched man that I am! Who will set me free from the body of this death? Thanks be to God through Jesus Christ our Lord!
> —ROMANS 7:23–25

The war is raging

Who will set us free from the body characterized by spiritual death? The soul and body are the scene of this spiritual confrontation. Sin living in our members, imparted with the fall of man in the Garden of Eden, brings spiritual death and separates us from our strongest desire: intimate fellowship with the Lord. As a result, man becomes aware that his strength alone is insufficient to win this war.

Paul appealed for the deliverance of his soul from the spiritual opposition working contrary to the true desire of his heart. The fallen nature of man is characterized by spiritual death—the performance of those things in opposition to his higher desire to do that which is good.

> Set your mind on things above, not on things on the
> earth. For you died, and your life is hidden with
> Christ in God.
>
> —COLOSSIANS 3:2–3 (NKJV)

Thanks be to God through Jesus Christ our Lord; we can
be free and experience victory in this battle as we surrender
to the fortifying work of God. Those who do are called
"overcomers." The Lord will have His overcoming victorious army who inherit the great promises reserved specifically for them. Our grace is the impartation of His heart of
desire to be fully submitted to the will of the Father and lib-
erated from the veils of separation.

Be slow to anger

The Holy Spirit has explicitly identified one of the great
strongholds of the enemy in the American Church to be anger.
Anger is generally the offspring of aggravation and irritation
promoted through the Western lifestyle permeating this
nation. The modern media fuels this fortress by promoting a
robust and stressful lifestyle, creating frustration and pressure,
even within Christian homes when allowed to succeed.

> This you know, my beloved brethren. But let every-
> one be quick to hear, slow to speak and slow to
> anger; for the anger of man does not achieve the
> righteousness of God.
>
> —JAMES 1:19–20

The strongholds must be identified and dealt with
through our biblical promises. To yield to these enemies is
not simply experiencing unwanted emotions. More seri-
ously, it admits demonic spirits assigned to create havoc and
confusion at every opportunity. Unresolved anger, left unad-
dressed, will become bitterness and will pervert our thinking

on every level. Bitterness will defile.

Thankfully, we have a remedy to free us from this snare that we may stand before the Lord with our soul sanctified. However, the spirit of anger will run rampant through the unsanctified soul as conditions in the earth become too much for many to handle. Multitudes of misguided people will turn to drugs, alcohol and prescription medication as a counterfeit remedy to settle their turbulent emotions.

Unresolved anger leads to depression and a spirit of confusion. We dwell in confusion continually when this evil opposition prevails. When unresolved anger, whether known or unknown, resides in our heart it causes us to hear communications through a demonic filter distorting comprehension and perception. It makes our hearing of the discourse and admonitions from others perverted and misconstrued, precipitating the hearing of one thing while we are expressing another.

These wrong perceptions amplify the division and separation of brothers that only fuel unresolved anger. It is imperative that we develop the spiritual insight that allows us to see Christ in each other and the important contributions we each make to the whole. Without one another functioning in the Body in our appointed place, the Body will be fragmented and incomplete.

Clear communication

If these strongholds are allowed to persist, it not only distorts our perception and communication with our brethren, but also misinterprets our view of the Lord and spawns an inaccurate image of Christ. We must see Him with an unveiled face in order to "behold and become."

But we all, with unveiled face, beholding as in a mirror the glory of the Lord, are being transformed into

the same image from glory to glory, just as from the Lord, the Spirit.

—2 CORINTHIANS 3:18

Unresolved anger, depression and bitterness are deep-seated veils clouding our view of the Lord and restricting our ability to be transformed into His image. These are areas of identification the Lord is desiring to address in His people during the coming season.

Over time, unresolved anger can actually mature into a root of bitterness which will completely defile. All manner of evil works result from a root of bitterness resulting in the depletion and destruction of our fruit.

Presently, there is an impartation of grace that allows us to identify the areas of unresolved anger, thus producing divinely granted repentance that frees us from the distortions and divisions created by this stronghold. It is important to point out that these identifications of enemy fortresses require a response on our part. It is by resisting and fleeing evil designs and calling upon the grace of God to extract carnal issues that the work of the Spirit is allowed to be complete.

The end result is open exchange with the Lord and true fraternal affection toward our brethren of every race, color and creed. This paves the way for the unity of the brethren that produces the oneness and wholeness greatly pleasing to the Lord. It opens the corridor that allows the release of His anointing from the resources of heaven.

Unity of the brethren

There is a specific and unique anointing that accompanies fraternal affection and unity of the brethren.

Behold, how good and how pleasant it is for brothers to dwell together in unity! It is like the precious oil

upon the head, coming down upon the beard, even
Aaron's beard, coming down upon the edge of his
robes. It is like the dew of Hermon, coming down
upon the mountains of Zion; for there the LORD com-
manded the blessing—life forever.

—PSALM 133:1–3

It is a noble pursuit for us to set our affections on heaven
and petition the Lord for an outpouring of His anointing. It
is an even higher purpose when brethren join together in
unity and affection as a corporate body having one voice
and asking for the intervention of God in the affairs of men.
This will produce a spirit of revival that will rejuvenate a
church or community with spirit and life.

The Lord will bless harmony among men even if diver-
sity and individuality exists. A state of perfection is not
required for the anointing to be imparted, only a heart of
sincerity and love. When a group becomes united in heart
and in His purposes, the Holy Spirit will deposit favor and
blessing among them.

Our divine purpose

We are living in the harvest generation. All the seeds
deposited in the Garden of Eden are coming to full maturity.
Both the seeds of darkness and the seeds of light are developing and requiring an active response on our part. This will
cause some who have straddled the spiritual fence to take
one side or the other.

We must be blistering hot, or else we will find ourselves
overcome by darkness. The times will no longer allow for
lukewarm Christianity. The spirit of Antichrist is coming to
full maturity in the earth. Likewise, the Spirit of Christ is
developing maturity in the hearts of many who will demonstrate the overcoming victory He achieved through mighty

expressions of spiritual authority and power.

The Lord has promised He is going to establish a biblical government with apostolic authority necessary for the preparation of His End-Time Church. That is the purpose for the identification of worldly fortresses within us and the extraction of their influence.

A great opportunity of grace is being released to the Church, if we will embrace it. This will begin the process of separating the precious from the worthless. The Lord can only trust us with the fullness of His power and authority when our character and nature is consistent with His.

The Holy Spirit is also stressing the importance of understanding spiritual authority if we are to fully comprehend the unfolding of His plan and the eminent release of His anointing. His governmental design will provide a new holy canopy of power and grace within the Church as the apostolic anointing and authority begin to be revealed with maturity. The true sign of maturity is found in the expression of His glory and His manifest "goodness." There will be a tangible presentation of His Person.

The apostolic anointing will function as a "cloud by day" and will serve as a "flaming fire" by night, providing a canopy of glory over believers who have been washed and purged by the "spirit of judgment" and the "spirit of burning." The prophet Isaiah foresaw this day and spoke of it.

> When the LORD has washed away the filth of the daughters of Zion, and purged the bloodshed of Jerusalem from her midst, by the spirit of judgment and the spirit of burning, then the LORD will create over the whole area of Mount Zion and over her assemblies a cloud by day, even smoke, and the brightness of a flaming fire by night; for over all the glory will be a canopy. And there will be a shelter to

give shade from the heat by day, and refuge and protection from the storm and the rain.

—Isaiah 4:4–6

The canopy of glory will provide shade from the heat of
judgment and a refuge and protection from the raging
storms of persecution and accusation. The Lord will be the
light of the canopy, and His glory will provide divine insula-
tion from the assaults of the adversary.

The victorious leaders in whom the refining process is
complete will be the "good shepherds" upon whom the
favor of the Lord will be apparent. They will mark the
restoration of the mature judges and counselors evident in
the early Church. These leaders will emerge, possessing the
mind of Christ and imparting Godly counsel essential for
our spiritual well-being.

Our previous lack of comprehension has greatly inhib-
ited our ability to be the bright shining light in this dark
world. This is beginning to change. The Lord is bringing
forth a people of great spiritual understanding who will
become beacons of light in the midst of deep darkness.

They will surface from this process anointed with Holy
Spirit power and displaying the Lord's victory over demons,
disease and death. This span of time we are experiencing is
providing a season of preparation and purging for the ones
being groomed for this anointing and commissioning. That
is the goal for which we set our sights as we lay aside all that
would stand in the way of this incredible destiny in which
we are privileged to participate.

Chapter 8

FORGETTING WHAT LIES BEHIND

To give undue attention to our personal past will only serve as a stumbling block to our desired goal of perfect fellowship with Him. The past contains both victories and defeats. The enemy will often try to divert our focus to either in an effort to draw our attention away from the Lord and our divine destiny.

> Brethren, I do not regard myself as having laid hold of it yet; but one thing I do: forgetting what lies behind and reaching forward to what lies ahead, I press on toward the goal for the prize of the upward call of God in Christ Jesus. Let us therefore, as many as are perfect, have this attitude; and if in anything you have a different attitude, God will reveal that also to you.
> —PHILIPPIANS 3:13–15

David, the great prophet and king, once said,

> One thing I have asked from the LORD, that I shall seek: That I may dwell in the house of the LORD all the days of my life, to behold the beauty of the LORD and to meditate in His temple.
> —PSALM 27:4

This singleness of purpose that is paramount is our pursuit to know God and walk intimately with Him. We can only allow ourselves to focus forward and upward in this noble quest to become one with Him. Anything else would serve only as a distraction from the "one thing" for which we have been called and commissioned.

Let us, therefore, so live that we may sincerely say, "There is one great object which we always have in view . . . *Him.*" With all diligence avoid everything which would interfere with that "one thing." The past is the past because it is the past. Let it thus remain.

Releasing His authority

In order for us to fulfill the commission to pull down strongholds and dominions holding captive our churches and communities, we must first experience freedom from the strongholds and dominions residing in us as individuals. Then, the necessary release of heavenly authority will be entrusted to destroy corporate fortresses of the enemy holding hostage our communities.

For now, a limited flow of power for ministry is being released. However, as love grows within us, greater measures of power will be bestowed with ever-increasing revelations of His glory. The Lord is the Spirit, and where the Spirit of the Lord is, there is liberty. The Lord is looking for "liberators" in whom He can display His glory and set the captive free.

The kingdom of heaven is within. Upon the thrones of our innermost being, He is to rule and reign, allowing the rivers of living water to flow freely, providing a refreshing to those who are perishing.

When the Lord Jesus entered the temple, He first drove out the moneychangers and robbers who defiled the temple with their corruption, confusion and excess. Then, the Scriptures record that the sick and afflicted were healed as they came to Him in His Temple.

> And they came to Jerusalem. And He entered the temple and began to cast out those who were buying and selling in the temple, and overturned the tables of the moneychangers and the seats of those who were selling doves; and He would not permit anyone to carry goods through the temple. And He began to teach and say to them, "Is it not written, 'My house shall be called a house of prayer for all the nations'? But you have made it a robbers' den."
>
> —MARK 11:15–17

We are to be His temple, and when the Holy Spirit comes in He will perform the same assignment, making us a "house of prayer." All we need to do is to give Him complete permission by the yielding of our will to the will of the Father. When we do He will drive out the corruption as He did the moneychangers from the literal temple.

We will love the Lord our God with our entire soul when it has been fully purified by the washing of the water of the Word. The divine attributes expressed to us through the Word provide the key that unlocks the resources of heaven to mold us and change us into His image, when applied in faith.

Having an absolute resolve in our hearts concerning this biblical heritage touches the heart of the Father, who releases grace and strength needed for the battle. We must have the determination to no longer allow these strongholds to separate and veil us from His presence and the fellowship that is rightfully ours.

> Therefore, strengthen the hands that are weak and the knees that are feeble, and make straight paths for your feet, so that the limb which is lame may not be put out of joint, but rather be healed. Pursue peace

with all men, and the sanctification without which no one will see the Lord.

—HEBREWS 12:12–14

The tares of our soul

A couple of years ago, I went through one of the most difficult seasons in recent memory. This trying time followed the release of several very encouraging prophetic words through a number of our highly regarded and respected prophetic friends. The words that were given involved our calling and commission along with many of the secret desires of our hearts that we were earnestly seeking.

During this troublesome time, it seemed that every base and carnal inclination was emerging to the forefront of my mind, seemingly consuming every thought and imagination. Overwhelming feelings of discouragement, rejection, anger and disappointment began to surface, making it difficult to pray or even study the Scriptures.

No matter what I tried, it did not seem to work. I employed every teaching I had learned over the years in overcoming assaults of the enemy that attempted to oppress my walk.

I rebuked everything that was pressing my mind. I recited the Scriptures in just the way I had learned, and I called upon the Lord to defend me against what I perceived to be an all-out assault of the enemy. When none of these techniques worked, I placed a desperate call to our prophetic friend Bob Jones.

When he answered, it seemed as though he were waiting for my call. The Lord had already spoken to him about the dilemma I was facing. When he told me the revelation he received from the Holy Spirit, I was surprised and dismayed. He shared how he had seen in a vision that the Lord was "pouring water on the tares of my soul." What an unusual expression!

The Lord was actually causing seeds of corruption that existed in my soul to begin to blossom and come to the forefront so they could be identified and dealt with. Then Bob said, "The tares of your soul are blossoming, and the Lord is sending the angels to gather them and remove them by the roots to be burned."

The Lord was causing the base nature to begin to blossom so I would call upon Him for mercy and grace for their removal. The merger of the Word and the Spirit provided the essential dynamics to bring divine life and illumination within my spirit that was necessary for the cleansing process.

It actually required action by the Holy Spirit for these issues to be recognized and appropriately dealt with. Many times, carnal issues remain hidden deeply within our soul, only to be exploited by our adversary at the pinnacle of our ministry in his attempt to shipwreck those called and anointed with divine purpose.

The mere recital of the Scriptures was not sufficient. This spiritual surgery required the anointing and revelation of the Spirit to quicken and make alive the Word of Truth necessary to replace the seeds of corruption with the dominion of His divine attributes.

Bob went on to say, "Do not faint; the first harvest is at hand." That seemed to me both good and bad news. It was good in that these oppressive and debilitating feelings would be extracted. The bad news was that it was the *first* harvest, indicating there would be others to follow. In reality, that was actually good news also, because it is the desire of our hearts to be thoroughly purged of the seeds of corruption that veil and separate us from the Lord and the walk of intimacy we desperately seek.

The harvest of tares

The admonition given to me during this difficult season

was to continue crying out to God for His mercy and grace to burn and consume all seeds of sin and corruption. I had often read the passage concerning the harvest of tares as it related to humanity, but I had never associated it with an individual life and the harvest of tares within us.

> **Allow both to grow together until the harvest; and in the time of the harvest I will say to the reapers, "First gather up the tares and bind them in bundles to burn them up; but gather the wheat into my barn."**
> **—MATTHEW 13:30**

Many within the body of Christ have been going through a similar process in order to achieve a place of heightened relationship and friendship with the Lord following this refining work. The Lord is looking for a house in which He can dwell and find rest. He is continuing to search for a place to rest His head. That will be the place of the revelation of His government. He does not merely desire to move through us . . . but to rest in us.

This process is essential for the dying of the old man and the emergence of the new, according to Galatians 2:20. For the many who embrace this process, the Lord is going to:

> **. . . [appoint] you over the nations and over the kingdoms, to pluck up and to break down: to destroy and to overthrow; to build and to plant.**
> **—JEREMIAH 1:10**

Bob then shared the encouraging word that came with his revelation:

> **Therefore, do not throw away your confidence, which has a great reward. For you have need of endurance, so that when you have done the will of God, you may receive what was promised. For yet in**

a very little while, He who is coming will come, and will not delay.

—HEBREWS 10:35–37

Our encouragement and the joy set before us is the inheritance of our promise—to be one with Him.

A divine opportunity

The Lord is now granting the divine opportunity to allow His Spirit to purge and extract every tendency toward corruption, becoming partakers of the divine nature, free from the corruption of this world and its lusts. As long as we walk in this world, housed in a tabernacle of flesh, we will continually need to "have our feet washed." However, that does not mean we must allow Satan to have a place of dominion and control over any department of our lives.

In John 14:30 the Lord announced that Satan was coming to Him, yet he (Satan) had no place in the Lord. In other words, there were no seeds of corruption to exploit in the Lord's nature. Satan had no dominion or doors of opportunity through which he could enter to cause corruption or collapse of the Father's purposes.

There was in the Lord no principle or feeling that agreed with Satan's, and nothing, therefore, by which he could prevail. Impurity only has power when there are some principles residing in us which are in agreement with the designs of the tempter, and which may be stimulated by presenting corresponding objects until our virtue is overcome. Where there is no such propensity, corruption has no power.

The Lord's spirit, soul and body were under the complete Lordship of the Father, thus allowing perfect fellowship with the Father that the Lord Jesus so earnestly cherished. The Scriptures promise we can likewise live in a blessed place through the awesome power of redemption and sanctification if we will willingly yield all the departments of our lives to His dominion.

Like the original seed

When the time came for the Lord to be glorified through the sacrificial offering of His life, He made it clear that His life was likened unto a grain of wheat. He taught that if this grain of wheat falls into the earth and perishes, it is for the purpose of bringing forth multiplied grains of wheat *like the original seed.*

> **Truly, truly, I say to you, unless a grain of wheat falls into the earth and dies, it remains by itself alone; but if it dies, it bears much fruit.**
>
> **—JOHN 12:24**

It is our high calling to emerge as one of the grains of wheat, like the original seed, who will begin to demonstrate and teach the kingdom design in the earth and walk before the Father with a purified spirit and soul.

There is a present move of the Holy Spirit to prepare a company of "overcomers" to *experience* the revelation of His kingship and give expression to that unveiling to the body of Christ, ushering in and birthing the kingdom of God in the earth.

The Bible teaches that when the Lord returns we are to be like Him. The Holy Spirit residing in us will reveal the same attributes through us that He did in the Lord Jesus Christ. He had perfect fellowship with the Father, and He is bringing forth "multiplied grains of wheat" like Himself who will know that level of intimacy with Him that He had with the Father. In fact, that is what we are commissioned to do. We are the vessels through which the light of God will shine into the midst of a dying earth.

PART IV

PUT ON THE LORD JESUS CHRIST

Chapter 9

GARMENTS OF SALVATION AND RIGHTEOUSNESS

THIS GENERATION HAS the exceptional privilege to live in a day in which the Lord is going to demonstrate Himself and His glory in ways never experienced in any prior age. The preparation of recent years has been to make ready a people for His own possession who will bear His image and exhibit His redemption. In order to carry the mantles of glory and power reserved for this company, we must have resident in us His divine nature and be adorned in His garments of salvation and righteousness.

I will rejoice greatly in the LORD, My soul will exult in my God; for He has clothed me with garments of salvation, He has wrapped me with a robe of righteousness, as a bridegroom decks himself with a garland, and as a bride adorns herself with her jewels.

For as the earth brings forth its sprouts, and as a garden causes the things sown in it to spring up, so the Lord GOD will cause righteousness and praise to spring up before all the nations.

—ISAIAH 61:10–11

Many of those called to leadership are presently being clothed with the attire of the "overcomer." These garments are designed specifically for our generation and are overwhelmingly adequate to overpower the spiritual darkness that the Scriptures point out will permeate the time of the end. It is not because we are more deserving than any prior age but more needy. Neither will it be because of any merits of our own, but because of His lovingkindness and compassion.

We are being molded and shaped to the very image necessary to carry these sacred garments provided by the Lord Himself. We are to be an extension of Him and His representation on earth. To do so, it is imperative that we allow the Holy Spirit to fashion us to be perfectly formed for the garments of the "overcomer."

Prophetically shown to many

This reality has been prophetically announced to a number of believers. Some have experienced dreams and visions displaying the removal of old filthy garments and the impartation of the new. Numerous others are receiving spiritual insight from the Scriptures or sense strong feeling of hunger and desire for more of the things of God.

Many truths are being imparted to the Church to help give clarity and understanding of this designing work. To gain understanding is to be chosen over silver, and it forms the foundation of life to the one who acquires it.

I recently had a sincere and devoted Christian friend share a revealing spiritual experience that provides great understanding of the way we are viewed in the realm of the spirit. In this unique prophetic revelation, the Holy Spirit allowed his eyes to be opened to both the natural and spiritual realms at the same time.

He was allowed to observe how the light within Christians provides a brilliant illumination easily recognized by the holy and unholy beings who reside in that domain. There is no need for us to wear a badge or announce our salvation for all the spirits to know we are Christians. We are described as the light of the world, and the salvation we have embraced adorns us in the light of heaven.

Furthermore, this experience permitted him to see how our emotions and internal qualities produce distinct light and smell easily discerned by both the angels and demons. For instance, if a person is dealing with anger or jealousy those emotions produce a unique color and scent that evil spirits recognize and exploit.

That is true of all the human emotions we confront. Likewise, divine attributes clothe us in the raiment and colors of heaven and the fragrance of His presence.

Great understanding is going to be delegated to the Bride of Christ in the coming days that will allow us to more fully understand the economy of heaven. Notable mysteries of the kingdom are soon to be committed to us, providing comprehension of the adornment of the Bride and the spiritual lights, sounds and fragrances they produce.

Discarding the old

We are very much like the prophetic picture depicted of Joshua the high priest in Zechariah 3. Although we stand before Him in the filthy garments of our own sin and failures, we are being given the awesome opportunity to be outfitted in His festal robes. When we learn to walk in His ways and perform His word, we will be given the opportunity to emerge as a governmental body and have authority in His house. Most importantly, we will be granted free access to His presence.

> **Now Joshua was clothed with filthy garments and standing before the angel. And he spoke and said to those who were standing before him saying, "Remove the filthy garments from him." Again he**

said to him, "See, I have taken your iniquity away from you and will clothe you with festal robes."

—ZECHARIAH 3:34

The old filthy clothing can represent a number of things, not the least of which are the traditions and doctrines of man that make the Word of God of no effect. The Lord cautioned against this error that substituted the precepts of man for the anointed Word of God. This will in effect nullify the grace of God.

We are living in a new day characterized by the manifestation and revelation of the kingdom of God in the earth. Fresh revelation from the heart of the Father is being introduced that will produce penetrating comprehension and illumination in the Scriptures, providing our meat in due season.

Put on Christ

The Lord is prophetically announcing His desire to "strip" us in order to clothe us with Himself and the garments of His righteousness. We are not going to be clothed with strikingly beautiful garments to the natural eye. Instead, it will be with a Spirit of humility:

You younger men, likewise, be subject to your elders; and all of you, clothe yourselves with humility toward one another, for GOD IS OPPOSED TO THE PROUD, BUT GIVES GRACE TO THE HUMBLE.

—1 PETER 5:5

These garments will only be beautiful to the spiritual eye and to the Lord. Being clothed in a spirit of humility and modesty will produce meekness, generating a teachable spirit capable of change into the very image of Christ.

But put on the Lord Jesus Christ, and make no
provision for the flesh in regard to its lusts.

—ROMANS 13:14

We are to put on Christ and make no provision for the
flesh in regard to its lusts. By submitting to Him and allowing this work to have its full benefit, we will be laying aside
all our fleshly desires and carnal inclinations. We thereby
make way to be clothed with the qualities, character and
attributes of Christ through His indwelling presence. There
is no other way to know the fullness of this reality than
through His abiding presence.

... put on the new self who is being renewed to a
true knowledge according to the image of the One
who created him—a renewal in which there is no distinction between Greek and Jew, circumcised and
uncircumcised, barbarian, Scythian, slave and free-
man, but Christ is all, and in all. And so, as those
who have been chosen of God, holy and beloved, put
on a heart of compassion, kindness, humility, gentleness and patience; bearing with one another, and for-
giving each other, whoever has a complaint against
anyone; just as the Lord forgave you, so also should
you. Beyond all these things put on love, which is the
perfect bond of unity.

—COLOSSIANS 3:10–14

Put on love

The most important teaching from these Scriptures is that
we clothe ourselves in love. Through divine love we will begin
to see the bond of unity that will produce the anointing. When
clothed with the anointing and His empowering presence, we
will make no provision for the flesh and its lusts.

The garment of love will increase our affection and

passion for Him first and foremost, allowing us to share in His love for others.

> . . . beyond all these things put on love, which is the perfect bond of unity.
>
> —COLOSSIANS 3:14

Ultimately, we are being transformed in order to be prepared to inherit the promises.

> For by these He has granted to us His precious and magnificent promises, in order that by them you may become partakers of the divine nature, having escaped the corruption that is in the world by lust.
>
> —2 PETER 1:4

"Galvanized" with Christ

We are to be "galvanized" with Christ. An iron chain is a very powerful tool; however, it is also notably prone to corruption and rust and thereby weakened. When the iron chain links have been "galvanized," they are coated with a layer of zinc that is non-corruptible. The chain links become much more powerful because they are not subject to corruption and rust and will endure under abusive conditions, such as salt water.

Living on the Gulf Coast and being a saltwater fisherman, I discovered this reality firsthand. The stoutest of our iron chains and equipment became brittle and vulnerable when continually exposed to the harshness of salt water and air. It soon became clearly apparent that all metals must be equipped with noncorruptible material or they could not be relied upon to meet the extreme challenges of a sometimes turbulent sea.

Likewise, our spirits, souls and innermost beings are to be "galvanized" with Christ and coated with His anointing.

Our corruptible traits will then be taking on His incorruptible nature, and we can escape the deterioration of this world and withstand the turbulent times ahead.

Demonstrated in servanthood

The Lord Jesus introduced into the world a new concept of greatness. It was to be found in humility and self-forgetting service. The Lord Himself stated that He did not come into the world to be ministered to . . . rather, He came into the world to minister to others and give His life as a ransom for many. That should also be our motivation as we strip ourselves of the selfish fleshly nature and put on the attitude resident in Christ.

Many people in these last days will be given the gifts and power to ambitiously extend their ministries internationally and develop a great name for themselves. They will also be given the choice to humbly esteem their gifts and become trustworthy stewards of the treasures entrusted to them.

The Lord illustrated His servant's heart by washing the feet of His disciples as an unforgettable lesson. He provided a divine example for us to follow. Then, in that place of willing submission, if our ministry touches the nations, it will only be according to His grace and provision.

He was the highest authority on earth with all power in heaven and on earth, yet He chose the path of humility and servanthood and demonstrated this truth to His disciples by taking upon Himself the most lowly of responsibilities, the washing of their feet.

Greatness in the kingdom of heaven is measured through humility and service.

> For who is greater, he who sits at the table, or he who serves? Is it not he who sits at the table? Yet I am among you as the One who serves.
>
> —LUKE 22:27 (NKJV)

The noblest evidence of true humility is demonstrated through obedience, simply doing those things which the Lord has asked us to do. His garments of salvation and righteousness will produce these qualities. Obedience genuinely is greater than sacrifice, and true servanthood is doing all that you can to help others achieve their calling and destiny in life.

Why the message of preparation

Throughout the Church one cry has uniformly echoed from the hearts of Gods people: "Send us Your power!" Without controversy, it is much needed. We will not attain our high calling and prophetic destiny without His empowering presence.

To that end we discover in Isaiah 11:2 an enlightening clue steering us to the release of the spirit of might and power. It is the accompanying spirit of counsel from the heart of the Lord providing a message of preparation for this great release.

> **And the Spirit of the LORD will rest on Him, the Spirit of wisdom and understanding, the Spirit of counsel and might, the Spirit of knowledge and of the fear of the LORD.**
>
> —ISAIAH 11:2 (NKJV)

In the Mt. Carmel showdown, Elijah was confronted and outnumbered by the many prophets of Baal who were leading Israel into rebellion and apostasy. When the prophets of Baal were unable to meet the challenge of Elijah, we notice the prophet carefully arranging the altar in a specific manner and meticulously following a prescribed order.

He first restored the altar of God that had been destroyed during the times of apostasy and then gathered twelve stones to represent God's governmental arrangement.

He followed up by pouring water on an altar that was to be consumed with fire—the opposite of what the natural mind would suggest. Nonetheless, he performed each task by the Lord's counsel.

> And it came to pass, at the time of the offering of the evening sacrifice, that Elijah the prophet came near and said, "LORD God of Abraham, Isaac, and Israel, let it be known this day that You are God in Israel and I am Your servant, and that I have done all these things at Your word."
>
> —1 KINGS 18:36 (NKJV)

Upon completion, Elijah declared he had done all those things by the Lord's instruction. Therefore, when he called upon the Lord for the demonstration of His power, the spirit of might was present to accompany the spirit of counsel released to Elijah in the preparation of the altar. The spirit of might supported and affirmed the careful obedience to the spirit of counsel followed by the prophet.

The Lord's counsel

In His admonition to this generation, the Lord gives us divine counsel. He advises us to buy from Him gold refined by fire that we may become rich, and white garments that the shame of our nakedness would not be revealed. He further instructs us to apply His eye salve that our eyes would be illumined to see the unseen.

By meticulously following the spirit of counsel, the spirit of power and might is dispersed to equip us as "overcomers" and qualify us to sit with Him on His throne as He overcame and sat with His Father on His. From this place, the Bride of Christ will emerge as priests and kings to appropriate the Lord's victory in the heavens and on earth.

> I advise you to buy from Me gold refined by fire, that you may become rich, and white garments, that you may clothe yourself, and that the shame of your nakedness may not be revealed; and eyesalve to anoint your eyes, that you may see. Those whom I love, I reprove and discipline; be zealous, therefore, and repent.
>
> Behold, I stand at the door and knock; if anyone hears My voice and opens the door, I will come in to him, and will dine with him, and he with Me.
>
> —Revelation 3:18–20

The Lord is standing at the door of our hearts sounding a prophetic voice, beckoning us to open to Him that He may dine with us. This is a call to our priestly ministry.

It was said of the Zadok priesthood that they remained faithful during times of infidelity. Because of their faithfulness, the Lord allowed a great privilege and set them apart to be drawn into His sanctuary to minister to Him and at His table. This passage provides a prophetic portrayal of our office as priests being given the great privilege to dine with the Lord and minister to Him.

> "But the Levitical priests, the sons of Zadok, who kept charge of My sanctuary when the sons of Israel went astray from Me, shall come near to Me to minister to Me; and they shall stand before Me to offer Me the fat and the blood," declares the Lord God. "They shall enter My sanctuary; they shall come near to My table to minister to Me and keep My charge."
>
> —Ezekiel 44:15–16

For those who willingly respond to His voice and His invitation for intimacy and fellowship, an impartation is granted to approve them to become "overcomers" and be allowed to

sit with Him on His throne as He overcame and sat with His
Father. Reclining with the Lord on His throne provides an indication of our kingly ministry to rule and reign with Him.

> **He who overcomes, I will grant to him to sit down**
> **with Me on My throne, as I also overcame and sat**
> **down with My Father on His throne.**
>
> **—REVELATION 3:21**

Resident in Revelation 3:20–21 is a call to both our
priestly and kingly ministries being granted to those who
overcome. The spirit of counsel is making ready a people to
be endowed with the spirit of might and positioned to enter
the "door standing open in heaven."

> **After these things I looked, and behold, a door stand-**
> **ing open in heaven, and the first voice which I had**
> **heard, like the sound of a trumpet speaking with me,**
> **said, "Come up here, and I will show you what must**
> **take place after these things."**
>
> **—REVELATION 4:1**

Chapter 10

PRIESTS AND KINGS

B Y "OVERCOMING" AND occupying our role as priests and kings we will first minister to Him in our heavenly role as priests. From that place of closeness and friendship we delegate the authority of Christ in the earth through our kingly position and begin to reveal the glory and power of His kingdom.

The administration of the priestly ministry equips and enables us relate to and affect the *heavenly* realm through worship, intimacy and relationship with the Lord. This divine office allows us to enter His sanctuary and draw near to His table and minister to Him by offering the sacrifices of praise, worship, intercession and mutual exchange. (See Ezekiel 44:14–16.)

The administration of the kingly ministry provides spiritual authority that allows us to relate to and influence the *earthly* realm as overcomers and delegate His victory and dominion achieved in His death and resurrection. Each of these ministries or divine offices has a specific function and related sphere of authority.

> **And they sang a new song, saying: "You are worthy to take the scroll, and to open its seals; for You were slain, and have redeemed us to God by Your blood out of every tribe and tongue and people and nation,**

And have made us kings and priests to our God; and
we shall reign on the earth."

—REVELATION 5:9–10 (NKJV)

Spirit of counsel and might

There is presently a message of preparation through the
spirit of counsel for those whom the Lord is grooming to
function in a governmental role, releasing the spirit of might
and power to bring judgment and dominion in the earth
through His delegated authority. This will be the establishing of His kingdom. We must seek first the kingdom of
heaven, which is both word and power expressed through:

> . . . living stones, [who] are being built up as a spiri-
> tual house for a holy priesthood, to offer up spiritual
> sacrifices acceptable to God through Jesus Christ.
>
> —1 PETER 2:5

This is in contrast to the prevailing thought of some that
we are strictly going to be "caught up" and experience the
kingdom only in heaven. The present work of grooming and
training will precede "the catching away," and relates to our
being empowered to rule in the earth by delegating the
Lord's victory before leaving the earthly realm.

We shall taste "the good word of God and the power of
the age to come" on this side of heaven as the Lord's enemies
are subdued and put under His feet. Then the Lord can come
for His Bride without spot or wrinkle and the restoration of
all things is accomplished. (See Acts 3:21.)

Reigning on earth

Revelation 5:10 introduces the song of the "overcomers"
and their responsibility as a royal race to rule as kings and
minister to Him as priests. Naturally, this passage points to
the millennial kingdom. However, to be ready for this great

purpose, there is a present "ruling" or overcoming in our lives being appropriated and manifested before we enter into the fullness of the millennial kingdom.

For this function to be fulfilled, we must become the habitation of God and His dwelling place. It will not merely be the Lord moving through us, but *resting in us*. This presents us in our priestly ministry. Then, as we begin to appropriate spiritual dominion and rule throughout the nations, we operate in our kingly ministry.

Crossing over to the promise

This is our promise and destiny as the dawning of a new day continues to ascend to the spiritual heights from which the priests and kings will become apparent. From this sacred place, anointed vessels will begin to function in their governmental capacity and appropriate the Lord's excellent victory. This is facilitated as we give ear to the spirit of counsel preceding the release of the spirit of might and power.

This ministry will produce fresh expressions of the wisdom of God, providing the blueprint and strategy designed for our overcoming victory. There are great and lofty things set aside for the End-Time generation. Spiritual pioneers will venture behind the veil to secure this insight and delegate divine wisdom in this hour.

Patterns and formulas

Much of what will be taking place in our generation will be unprecedented displays of His kingdom work. Old patterns and formulas heretofore relied upon will not have the favor and blessing of God as they perhaps have in prior expressions of outpouring. One of the hardest things for man is to relinquish the good in order to welcome the best.

> Brethren, I do not regard myself as having laid hold of it yet; but one thing I do: forgetting what lies

behind and reaching forward to what lies ahead, I
press on toward the goal for the prize of the upward
call of God in Christ Jesus.

—PHILIPPIANS 3:13–14

Clearly, this is not implying that we abandon founda-
tional truth, but rather the tendency to mold fresh outpourings of His Spirit into old methods and techniques with
which we are accustomed. We sometimes become comfortable with the familiar, and it can easily become a crutch.

The Holy Spirit is preparing a company of "pioneers"
who will advance over to the deep things of God and
demonstrate them to this generation. A pioneer is one who
opens or prepares the way for others to follow. They will be
exemplified in a "John-the-Baptist-type" ministry. These
will be a "voice" of another and will know the reality of
Jeremiah 33:3 by calling upon Him to show us great and
mighty things which we do not presently know.

This process will establish the "royal priesthood"
prophetically illustrated in Zechariah 3 and the transformation of Joshua the High Priest. The Lord Jesus is the Head,
and we are to be His body and must be "bone of His bone
and flesh of His flesh."

Let Your priests be clothed with righteousness, and
let Your saints shout for joy.

—PSALM 132:9 (NKJV)

The giants of the land

The enemies that inhabit the "promised land" are the
strongholds and dominions existing in our soul that must be
overcome through the appropriation of the blood of Christ
and His victory. These enemies are too great for us in our
own strength, just as the inhabitants of the Promised Land

were too great for Israel to defeat without the Lord's supernatural intervention.

Although ten of the spies returned with evil reports, it remained the decision of the people to choose which report they believed. They could have chosen to believe the faithful report of Joshua and Caleb. In so doing, they would have experienced the great power of "Captain of the Lord's Host" and enjoyed the fullness of their promise.

So is it with us today. Although the strongholds and worldliness in us seems insurmountable, the Lord has pledged in His Word that we have the precious and magnificent promises by which we can become partakers of the divine nature and escape the corruption of this world and its lusts. Our part is in yielding to the Holy Spirit and allowing this work to be realized.

Chapter 11

THE KEYS TO
THE KINGDOM

To be ambassadors for Christ and His representation on the earth, we must be trustworthy stewards of the power and authority that accompanies the "keys to the kingdom." This can be achieved only when we share in the Lord's nature and character by overcoming the corruption that presently exists in our soul.

When we allow the Holy Spirit to reveal and extract the seeds of corruption, it will produce the necessary character and divine attributes that make us candidates not only to be called, but also to be chosen and sent. That is the message His voice is proclaiming as he stands at the door of our hearts and knocks, searching for those who will open to Him and dine.

Tokens of this reality

The Lord has given "tokens" of this reality through individuals who crossed over as spies and returned with the fruit of this land and shared it with the body of Christ. These individuals have been "prototypes" of an entire company of people who are to function in a governmental role equipped with the "keys of the kingdom," having tasted the good word of God and the power of the age to come.

Some have already lived their life of victory and entered their reward, such as John G. Lake and Maria Woodworth-Etter. Others are presently emerging, having tasted this reality.

Although there were a number of ministers sharing the gospel of healing and salvation around the turn of the twentieth century, Maria Woodworth-Etter seemed to possess a ministry of revelation and power that touched a far deeper dimension in God. She and many in her meetings were given astounding visions and revelations including insight into the perfecting of God's Bride and events surrounding the End-Time generation.

She did not simply carry a gift of healing but functioned in kingdom principles, providing a blanket of glory that often visited her meetings. It was reported by many witnesses that the power that accompanied her would touch many for miles around who were not even in her meetings.

The saved and sinners alike were often overcome by the power of God and given visions and trances of both heaven and hell as they walked the streets of the cities she was visiting. I have in my possession numerous confirmations of this reality, including newspaper clippings from meetings held in Meridian, Mississippi, the place of my birth. Secular journalists provided written reports of astounding miracles and power witnessed in her meetings.

In her journals, Woodworth-Etter chronicled God's early dealings with her and the commission she carried. She openly testified of the refining process of the beginning years that molded and shaped her for the place in God she would dwell. Perhaps the seemingly harsh dealings could have been lessened with more cooperative decisions. However, she, like Dowie and Lake, was a pioneer and didn't have the life lessons to guide her as we do in the examples of these generals of the faith.

She once reported how the Lord stood face-to-face with her and assured her of His favor and blessing to carry the kingdom message to her generation. She recorded, "There appeared upon the wall a large open Bible, and the verses stood out in raised letters. The glory of God shown around the book. I looked, and I could understand it all. Then Jesus said again, 'Go, and I will be with you.'"[1]

She further recounted how she learned more in that single divine experience than she could have comprehended with many years of diligent study. Naturally, we must continually study to show ourselves approved. However, close encounters with God, like the one this precious sister was given, will take us to heightened levels of understanding of the mysteries of the kingdom and God's written Word.

She went on to record, "I want the reader to understand that, at this time, I had a good experience, a pure heart and was full of the love of God, but was not qualified for God's work. I knew that I was but a worm. God would have to take a worm to thresh a mountain. Then I asked God to give me the power He gave the Galilean fishermen—to anoint me for service. I came like a child asking for bread. I looked for it. God did not disappoint me. The power of the Holy Ghost came down like a cloud. It was brighter than the sun. I was covered and wrapped in it. I was baptized with the Holy Ghost and fire and power, which has never left me. There was liquid fire, and the angels were all around me in fire and glory."[2]

The Holy Spirit has plainly shown us Maria Woodworth-Etter was a "spy" or "token" of one who tasted the power of the age to come and introduced the fruit of that land to her generation and ours.

A recent token

While in a prophetic conference in Kelowna, BC, Canada, during the summer of 2001, a precious sister who is a missionary to Mozambique participated in the conference. She spoke from her heart with the attendees and shared recent experiences she had had with the Lord as He pruned and prepared her. As she did, the Holy Spirit spoke to me and revealed that she was like one of the spies who ventured over into the promised land and returned with portions of the fruit of the land. As some introduce kingdom fruit and divine promise, it remains up to the people to choose to believe or reject the report.

Her message was likewise one of preparation as she disclosed how the Lord "glued" her to the floor for seven days and seven nights, moving through her with waves of His Spirit, revealing areas and issues that were contrary to His nature.

Much took place during this season, but the end result was the death to self and soulish motives and agendas. From that place of surrender she was allowed to embrace His Spirit as a dwelling place, allowing total dominion in her spirit, soul and body, according 1 Thessalonians 5:23. Tremendous miracles, signs and wonders began to emerge in her ministry with countless reports of healings and creative miracles as sight was restored, lame limbs were given strength, and cancers were healed.

The spirit of Elijah

The Lord Jesus Himself made a unique prophetic promise that, "Elijah is coming and will restore all things." Furthermore, He acknowledged that Elijah had already come. The Lord was clearly pointing to the prophetic promise of Malachi 4 concerning this notable anointing.

> And His disciples asked Him, saying, "Why then do the scribes say that Elijah must come first?" And He answered and said, "Elijah is coming and will restore

all things; but I say to you, that Elijah already came, and they did not recognize him, but did to him whatever they wished. So also the Son of Man is going to suffer at their hands." Then the disciples understood that He had spoken to them about John the Baptist.

—MATTHEW 17:10–13

Naturally, the disciples understood that He was referring to John the Baptist as they regarded the past expression of this prophetic mandate. The Scriptures plainly point out that this prophet was anointed with the spirit and power of Elijah.

According to the commission announced through Gabriel, John was to direct the hearts of the fathers to the children. He was to point the hearts of the fathers of Israel to the birthing of a new thing. It was a new beginning for the covenant people of God.

Behold, I am going to send you Elijah the prophet before the coming of the great and terrible day of the LORD. And he will restore the hearts of the fathers to their children, and the hearts of the children to their fathers, lest I come and smite the land with a curse.

—MALACHI 4:5–6

There are two distinct objectives expressed in Malachi 4:6 regarding the dispersal of the spirit of Elijah: to turn the hearts of the fathers to their children and to restore the hearts of the children to their fathers.

John the Baptist was considered to be the Lord's forerunner who prepared a company of people for the Lord and His message. Careful scrutiny of Luke 1:17 reveals that Gabriel only expressed one portion of Malachi 4:6, involving the turning of the hearts of the fathers to the children. He was to direct disobedient and incredulous hearts to the wisdom and knowledge discovered in the loving will of God and to make ready a people perfectly prepared and set apart for the Lord.

There will be a subsequent release of this anointing that will accomplish the remainder of the prophetic admonition and restore the hearts of the children to the fathers. That is, the restoration of a company of people to the heart of devotion and dedication resident in our apostolic fathers.

This outpouring will immediately precede God's judgment that will be burning like an oven, consuming the proud and arrogant. Peter also foresaw and wrote of this day. According to Malachi, the enemies of God will be like stubble, fully consumed as ashes under the feet of the righteous. This has not yet been fulfilled.

Preparation and restoration

The spirit of Elijah is a ministry of preparation and restoration. It is the readiness of a company of people to receive the ingrafted Word and become living expressions of it. It is also the ministry of recovery that reconciles us to a place once lost. Primarily, it is the restoration of our purpose to be a people for God's own possession with whom He has intimate exchange and relationship and through whom He will fill the earth with His glory.

Throughout Church history, the Lord has always had a remnant of people loyal to Him who lived separate and devoted lives of consecration and commitment. Many documents and books are provided that record the lives of these saints, such as Polycarp, Irenaeus, Columba, John Wesley and many others.

Much is written about their walk with God and the awesome experiences and face-to-face encounters they enjoyed. Their life of surrender to the will of God was marked with powerful demonstrations of the Spirit and His power. Miracles, signs and wonders were commonplace and vindicated the Lord's message for their generation. It would put us to shame to read of their willingness to be living sacrifices and tabernacles of His holy attributes.

Nonetheless, we discover in the Scriptures that Elijah was a man like us with like passions. Paul taught that there is not any good thing in us. How do we cross this chasm from where we are to where we need to be?

This gulf is bridged with desire—a desire to be yielded vessels who truly know the Lord Jesus. It requires a direct impartation of the grace of God to be clothed in His garments of purity and righteousness. That is the heart of devotion that was resident in our fathers. It will be imparted to a desperate company of people who will not be denied their opportunity to become the friends of God.

> **To this end also we pray for you always that our God may count you worthy of your calling, and fulfill every desire for goodness and the work of faith with power; in order that the name of our Lord Jesus may be glorified in you, and you in Him, according to the grace of our God and the Lord Jesus Christ.**
>
> **—2 THESSALONIANS 1:11–12**

Our prophetic promise is that a generation will know the restoration and impartation of the heart of desire for God that existed in these saints and propelled them to great heights in the Spirit.

A prophetic reaffirmation

The Holy Spirit recently allowed a prophetic experience that I believe suggests the present release of the Spirit of Elijah for our day. While praying for people during the close of a prophetic conference early in 2002, my eyes were opened to the dimension of the Spirit, and I beheld a door being opened in heaven. Immediately upon its opening, mighty warring angels proceeded through the door headed to the earth.

I was not able to count their number, but it was a significant company of the most awesome warriors imaginable. Following their release, I watched a single chariot of fire proceed through the door as if dispatched from heaven. I believe the chariot of fire represented the spirit of Elijah being delegated to us to be expressed through the vessels groomed and prepared for this anointing.

When Wanda and I returned home that evening from the conference, the Lord provided a wonderful affirmation of the revelation. We felt compelled to call Bob Jones and report to him the events of the weekend and determine if the Holy Spirit had spoken insight regarding the events of recent days.

Before I could even share with him the things that had taken place, he began to communicate a visitation he received that morning from an angelic warrior. He reported that the heavenly warrior was one of the highest-ranking angels he had ever encountered, and he functioned directly under the authority of Michael. Interestingly, Bob observed that the angel spoke with him in a Celtic accent that seemed to have a prophetic message in itself.

The angelic warrior announced to Bob that warring angels are being dispatched to help us in the fulfillment of our commission for this hour. His visitation was an incredible affirmation of the open door and spiritual release of ministering spirits to fortify us and pave the way for the manifestation of the spirit and power of Elijah. We must be prepared for this appointment.

PART V

BEING CLOTHED
WITH CHRIST

Chapter 12

THE BATTLEFIELD VISION

WHILE AT A prophetic conference in Charlotte, North Carolina, the Lord graciously imparted a vision of the night that relates the essence of our need for refinement and equipping. I share it in hopes that it will also provide further clarity to the message the Lord desires that we embody.

In the vision, the army of light was aligned in an open field, standing in battle formation and about to engage the army of darkness. Throughout the ranks, soldiers of light were admirably clothed in ancient battle armor, each having a sword in his hand.

When the battle ensued it was intensely aggressive in what we perceived was the great "End-Time battle." With each blow of our swords, we were seemingly driving the enemy back to what appeared to be a sure victory for us.

Although the fighting was forceful and even brutal, persistent progress was being made as we continued to press the enemy and steadily take ground. Because of our ability to push the enemy back, we perceived that we were winning the "End-Time" confrontation and were suitably equipped for this great battle.

Withstood by the Holy Spirit

Suddenly, the Holy Spirit arrested us and would not allow us to advance any further. There was a feeling of shock and dismay as we were halted in our battle progress, not by the enemy, but by the Holy Spirit. As I was standing directly before our enemy only a few yards away, I was seemingly paralyzed and unable to advance.

Confused and dismayed, I asked the Lord why He was withstanding us. With that question, the Lord caused the clouds above to part, and our eyes were opened to the great and massive "guns" of the enemy that were hidden and leveled in our direction.

In reality, we were not driving the enemy back because of our great strength. Rather, we were allowed by the enemy to push them back as a deception to imply that we were equipped for the battle. In the condition that we remained in the battlefield, we possessed a measure of strength and virtue imparted to us through our walk with the Lord. However, we did not embody the full dimension of His provision essential for this long foretold conflict.

One of the things most adamantly opposed by the enemy is the complete release of His Spirit upon the Church. Our adversary knows that when God's people are anointed with the prophetic mandate to be clothed with the fullness of His revelation and power, we will return to the Lord, and He will heal us. That healing will not merely consist of physical and emotional restoration, but it will also fully mend the breach that has existed between God and man since the Garden of Eden.

Once accomplished, the reality of "Christ in us—the hope of glory" becomes apparent, and we walk in the prophetic destiny foretold in the Scriptures. That explains why there has been so much opposition to this emerging prophetic generation.

The enemy recognizes that his only chance for victory is to entice us into battle prematurely. Once the bride of Christ obtains the revelation of the whole measure of Christ and enters that place of habitation, the enemy will have no chance for victory. In that place we can stand alone as a raid against all the forces of hell, not because of our own strength, but because we are drawing on the unseen resources of heaven and His ultimate overcoming victory.

It was the mercy and grace of God that we were not allowed to advance any farther. It would have been to our demise. The Father's love is so great, He will not allow us to enter this conflict without first having the opportunity to be fully clothed with Christ and the armor of His provision. If we had advanced any farther, the massive weapons of the enemy released for the great End-Time battle would have easily destroyed us.

The operating room

With this discovery, we were transported to what symbolically appeared to be a heavenly operating room and training facility. Uniquely, in this extraordinary room, I was both lying on the operating table and also standing behind the angels who surrounded the table. I watched as they prepared to do "surgery."

There were perhaps six to eight angels standing approximately seven feet tall and encircling the table. Each worker was intently focused on the task at hand, namely, to perform the spiritual "surgery" essential for us to be prepared for our eminent battle.

The attendants in the room immediately began to "strip" layer after layer of flesh, removing the issues of carnality and worldly conformity. I watched as my own identities, agendas, ambitions and desires were extracted and discarded. I was permitted to understand that there is no place for mixture in the coming battle. We cannot allow the leaven of our own thoughts and ideas to be injected into the purity of His truth. It must be untouched by the hands of man.

This process continued until I finally peered over the shoulder of one of the angels and asked the question, "Where am I, for I no longer see myself?" A voice spoke, pointing to a small yet vibrant seed of life that remained on the table. All that was allowed to exist after their deliberate work was the impartation of life given to me from God.

This stripping process had, in essence, carried us back to the very origin of life, removing all fleshly attributes born in the Garden of Eden with the fall of man. This was done to enable us to "put on Christ" and become spiritually qualified to stand victorious in battle with the armies of darkness.

Flesh of His flesh

The attendants began the assignment of putting us back together, now using divinely powerful attributes that were mighty in God and adequate for the awesome battle. The angels undertook the reconstruction procedure with the same vigor and determination as the stripping process. Except now, the materials were "bone of His bone and flesh of His flesh." Any preparation other than the one described here would result in certain defeat.

> Finally, be strong in the Lord, and in the strength of His might. Put on the full armor of God, that you will be able to stand firm against the schemes of the devil.
>
> —Ephesians 6:10–11

When the restoration process was complete, we were returned to the battlefield. Now, in lieu of having a sword in our hands, we *were* the sword or weapon in the Lord's hand. Instead of having a "promise," we *became* the promise.

The sword in Scripture is indicative of the Word of promise. Presently, we are attempting to battle the enemy with our promises. It is the Lord's intent to *make* us the promise. We are to become the Living Word.

> But put on the Lord Jesus Christ, and make no pro-
> vision for the flesh in regard to its lusts.
>
> —ROMANS 13:14

Christian us

One of the greatest mysteries that will be fully realized is the wonder of Christ in us, the hope of glory. We recite the words but very few experientially discover the absolute and complete reality. However, the Scriptures have promised that an entire company of believers will soon emerge anointed with this certainty. They will walk in the fullness of truth with great power and authority and, more importantly, radiate the nature and character of Christ through His manifested glory.

For the many being enlisted in the Lord's army, this transformation process is presently taking place. The new divinely powerful make-up represents the increased dimension of the spirit of revelation and power, enabling us to call upon Him that He would answer us and show us great and mighty things which we presently do not know. This will provide the heavenly strategy and blueprint for ultimate victory.

A number of saints are being given spiritual experiences that feature themselves being stripped and re-clothed with brighter and more glorious garments as we enter this new day in the Spirit and progress from glory to glory.

> But we all, with unveiled face beholding as in a mir-
> ror the glory of the Lord, are being transformed into
> the same image from glory to glory, just as from the
> Lord, the Spirit.
>
> —2 CORINTHIANS 3:18

The audible voice

An audible voice then spoke in the vision declaring, "The weapons set against you are much more powerful than you ever imagined! The divinely powerful weapons provided for you are also far more powerful than you ever imagined."

One of the foremost strategies of the enemy in this hour is to deceive the Church into thinking we are properly equipped for the coming battle. The enemy knows his only opportunity for victory can result by keeping us from the absolute realization of God's provision. This birthright can only be released when we allow the Holy Spirit to purge the carnal nature and align with Christ as one spirit, becoming a recipient of the divine nature. (See 2 Peter 1:4.)

When this occurs, the Lord finds His abode in us, living out His life through us in perfect union. The cost is great, death to self, yet the reward is exceedingly greater than our human minds can comprehend.

Chapter 13

EXAMINED BY
THE WORD

THERE IS PRESENTLY an examination that is taking place: an evaluation of the condition of our spirit according to the revelation of His Word for our generation. The inspection will determine our spiritual ability to engage the enemy on the Lord's behalf. There is a creative Word being released in God's person that is refining and preparing us for the coming war.

It is through His Word abiding in us and merged with the Spirit that provides the armor of salvation and righteousness that will clothe and equip us for the battle. Any other spiritual raiment will only become obstacles and opportunities for the enemy. That is, if we are carrying traditions, doctrines and perceptions of men rather than the true revelation of the Word, those doctrines will surely become cumbersome weights that interfere with our ability to meet the challenge of the new day.

> Therefore gird up the loins of your mind, be sober, and rest your hope fully upon the grace that is to be brought to you at the revelation of Jesus Christ.
> —1 PETER 1:13 (NKJV)

Our spirit and soul are to be girded with truth. The Spirit

of Truth will provide the strength and power essential for the overcoming army to be dressed and prepared to take the ground allotted for us.

The Lord Jesus once said, "I have food to eat you know not of." This was clearly speaking of a spiritual provision that afforded the nourishment and strength He needed to meet the challenges of His day and fulfill the great call on His Life. Likewise, our spiritual man must continually be maintained with the "bread" that continually proceeds from the heart of the Father.

The spirit of wisdom and revelation

Ephesians 1:17–18 emphasizes the right of every believer to be anointed with the spirit of wisdom and revelation. This form of wisdom is not merely the ability to mentally analyze a situation and make a good response. Rather, it is a spiritual endowment that allows a believer to go deep into the heart of the Father to perceive and understand the mysteries of the kingdom and our rights through redemption. Not only do we have the liberty to understand these mysteries but also the accompanying spirit of revelation that gives illumination and comprehension of their reality.

> . . . the God of our Lord Jesus Christ, the Father of glory, may give to you a spirit of wisdom and of revelation in the knowledge of Him. I pray that the eyes of your heart may be enlightened, so that you may know what is the hope of His calling, what are the riches of the glory of His inheritance in the saints, and what is the surpassing greatness of His power toward us who believe.
>
> —EPHESIANS 1:17–19

The spirit of wisdom is more clearly defined as a supernatural impartation of the Spirit, granting the ability to see

and recognize the Lord Jesus with a spiritual knowledge and
comprehension of His mysteries, plans and purposes. This
heritage will reveal the manifold and unsearchable wisdom
and secrets of God hidden in Christ. It relates to a deeper
intimacy and awareness into the things of God and intimates
a close personal encounter with the Lord.

The accompanying spirit of revelation grants a comprehension of these mysteries and attributes of God. It involves
an understanding and perception with our soul of these
things revealed in the spirit. It grants the ability not only to
know the things of God but also the practical application of
them in the earth and in our lives.

The apostle Paul was anointed, and he flowed with this
spirit as he continually conveyed the mysteries of the kingdom to his generation. This same spirit is essential for us in
this generation to know the concealed secrets reserved for
the last days and share in the hidden manna set aside for the
End-Time perfecting of the Bride.

> But as for you, Daniel, conceal these words and seal
> up the book until the end of time; many will go back
> and forth, and knowledge will increase.
> —DANIEL 12:4

Walking in the full measure of Christ

The spirit of wisdom and revelation provides three distinct blessings essential for our ability to walk in the full
measure of Christ through the eyes of our heart that are
being flooded with the light of understanding: That we may
know 1) what is the hope of His calling; 2) what are the
riches of the glory of His inheritance in the saints; 3) what is
the surpassing greatness of His power toward us who believe.

When we read these words, our intellectual minds detect
they are great promises that have been provided. Even so,

when anointed with the spirit of wisdom and revelation, we obtain an experiential comprehension of our redemptive birthright. It becomes living truth, given expression through consecrated vessels.

As the Scriptures point out, eye has not seen, ear has not heard, nor has it entered into the heart of man all the great blessings the Lord has provided for us. Nevertheless, to a called and set-apart people, it has been granted to know the mysteries of the kingdom. The spirit of wisdom and understanding provides the articulation and comprehension of His "glorious inheritance in the saints."

The Spirit of Truth

One of the issues of great importance that has been consistently emphasized by the Lord during this season of the Spirit, is the full manifestation of the Spirit of Truth. As the emerging army of believers, we must learn to embrace truth that the "fog" of deception and delusion can no longer have its way in the Church. As we "gird our loins" with the "belt of truth," our foundation in Christ is firmly established, allowing for the full release of His anointing for our End-Time commission.

In the correction to the Laodiceans, the Church that most appropriately describes this generation, the Lord announces our delusion that we are rich and increased in goods, having need of nothing. However, that is a deception. Viewed from heaven's perspective, she is wretched, miserable, poor, blind and naked.

This reproof clearly identifies the spirit of deception as one of the prevalent defiling fortresses during this generation. We must overcome this enemy if we are to sit with Him on His throne, as He overcame and sat with the Father. In fact, we shall overcome this enemy. John foresees this victory as he is allowed to admire the devoted Bride in all her beauty, adorned for the King.

In order to overcome the enemy and his deceptions, as the Lord did when led by the Spirit into the wilderness, we must also share in His divine nature and character to confront the same counterfeit appeals. We are not adequate in our strength to triumph over the deceiver. It is only in the Lord's strength that we are made strong and equipped to prevail over all the enemy can deliver.

The plan of the enemy is to utilize the spirit of deception and delusion in the arena of the spirit, soul and body. The instrument of his destruction will be the deceiving spirit that would convey that we are in one condition when in reality we are in another, or attempt to sidetrack us on detours and dead-ends. If he can deceive us in this manner, it would cause us to go into combat without being fully equipped for the battle.

All the forces of hell will be released against the Church in the great End-Time battle. His only opportunity for victory is to attempt to seduce the Church into entering the battle while lacking the full armor of the Spirit.

Our promise is to be like the Lord. He is the firstfruit among many brethren. When the grain of wheat falls into the ground and dies, it is for the purpose of producing multiplied grains of wheat like the original seed. In order to win the contest ahead, we must be like Him. That is our promise and our destiny. We cannot settle for anything less.

> **Beloved, now we are children of God, and it has not appeared as yet what we shall be. We know that, when He appears, we shall be like Him, because we shall see Him just as He is.**
>
> **—1 JOHN 3:2**

One of the admonitions given to the Laodicean church was to be clothed in white garments, that the shame of their nakedness would not be revealed. The white garments represent priestly and divinely powerful apparels by which we cover ourselves spiritually. It is very important that each person go through this process to receive the garments provided by the Holy Spirit, specifically designed and created for our individual calling and purpose.

I advise you to buy from Me gold refined by fire so that you may become rich, and *white garments, that you may clothe yourself,* and that the shame of your nakedness may not be revealed; and eyesalve to anoint your eyes, that you may see.
—REVELATION 3:18 (EMPHASIS ADDED)

Our ultimate invitation is to be like Him and display His armor of righteousness, sanctification, revelation and power.

I will rejoice greatly in the LORD, my soul will exult in my God; for He has clothed me with garments of salvation, He has wrapped me with a robe of righteousness, as a bridegroom decks himself with a garland, and as a bride adorns herself with her jewels.
—ISAIAH 61:10

The Lord is presently examining His army of believers to determine if the condition of their spirit is adequately suited for the challenges of the coming battle. The advancing season of the Spirit will allow substantial fruitfulness and restoration for those who are spiritually mature and strengthened to become trustworthy stewards of His mysteries and power.

If we do not cultivate a love for the truth, especially in the season ahead, we will be turned over to a spirit of delusion.

. . . the one whose coming is in accord with the activity of Satan, with all power and signs and false wonders, and with all the deception of wickedness

for those who perish, because they did not receive the
love of the truth so as to be saved. And for this rea-
son God will send upon them a deluding influence so
that they might believe what is false . . .

—2 THESSALONIANS 2:9–11

Unfortunately, many erroneous doctrines continue to be
embraced in the Church, providing veils that separate us
from the One we seek. A powerful release of the Spirit of
Truth is coming to guide us into *all truth*, dispelling the lies
taught as truth and providing a sanctifying light.

PART VI

THE APOSTOLIC IS COMING

Chapter 14

OUR INVITATION

THERE IS CURRENTLY an invitation to meet with the Lord in the Holy Place for intimate relationship. In the pattern prophetically illustrated by the Holy Place in the Tabernacle of Moses, introduction is made and development inaugurated for an even higher place. In this sacred domain, preparation is secured to fortify the Lord's priests to enter the most holy of all places, the Holy of Holies and union with God.

Although the veil separating the two was rent by the Lord's crucifixion, great reverence and awe surround this place in God. One dare not enter the Most Holy Place until full understanding of the instruments in the Holy Place are residing deep within the believer. The priesthood established by Moses fully understood this reality.

> For there was a tabernacle prepared, the outer one, in which were the lampstand and the table and the sacred bread; this is called the holy place. And behind the second veil, there was a tabernacle which is called the Holy of Holies, having a golden altar of incense and the ark of the covenant covered on all sides with gold, in which was a golden jar holding the manna, and Aaron's rod which budded, and the tables of the covenant.
>
> —HEBREWS 9:2–4

One of the predominant colors woven into the linen used in the Holy Place is blue. Blue is typically symbolic of revelation and illumination of the heavenly design. The blue colors incorporated in the various parts of the tabernacle described in Exodus 25–27 were intended while on earth to remind Israel of their heavenly revelation and purpose.

It is in the Holy Place that we are able to sit at His feet and partake of Him through the revelation of His nature and character by the light of His Spirit. The invitation is to come by revelation into the Holy Place to become acquainted with the Lord Jesus Christ.

The Lord's aspiration for us is freedom so we can partake of the intimate relationship He longs to have with His people. This objective has always been the heart of the Father: to have a people for His own possession with whom He can have relationship and through whom He can express His divine attributes.

The lampstand

In the Holy Place, one of the first instruments we are able to observe is the lampstand.

This is representative of light being shed abroad in our hearts to illumine the revelation of the Lord. He is lighting our candle to enlighten our dark places.

For You will light my lamp; the LORD my God will enlighten my darkness.

—PSALM 18:28 (NKJV)

Without His light, we are blinded by the spirit of this world to our true condition and the riches of our inheritance in Him. Foremost in our birthright is the opportunity, through his great grace, to be free from our carnality and sins that so easily beset us and separate us from Him.

... the god of this world has blinded the minds of the unbelieving, that they might not see the light of the gospel of the glory of Christ, who is the image of God. For God, who said, "Light shall shine out of darkness," is the One who has shone in our hearts to give the light of the knowledge of the glory of God in the face of Christ.

—2 CORINTHIANS 4:4, 6

The lampstand was fashioned from a single block of gold and was the only source of light in the Holy Place. It was fueled by pure olive oil, symbolically speaking of His anointing to enlighten us to the deceptions of the world and our own lusts. (See Zechariah 4:1–7.) Our present invitation is to enter the Holy Place and allow the light of His Spirit to shine upon our seeds of corruption so they can be uprooted as we cry to Him for deliverance.

As we allow this process, we will likewise receive the impartation of the attributes that are essential to enter *and maintain* His divine presence without grieving His Holy Spirit.

Once our conscience is clear and we are walking in the light, we likewise become the light of the world as Jesus described in Matthew 5:14–16. We can shine for the Lord in the midst of this dark and corrupt generation. His light resident in us will draw others to Him, not because of any virtue of our own but because of His manifestation in us. (See Philippians 2:15.) That is the gospel of Jesus Christ: Christ in us, the hope of glory.

When the candlestick was lighted it produced illumination in the Holy Place. When our candle has been lighted it will produce an illumination and glory that will emanate from us as described in the life of Peter. The Scriptures portray Peter so clothed in the glory of God that the mere casting of the glory-shadow over the people produced healing and allowed them to touch the resources of heaven for their great needs. The sevenfold Spirit of God resting in us will provide the same great illumination that will make us the exceptional light that shines in dark places.

The bread of His presence

Man does not live by bread alone but by every word that continually proceeds from the mouth of God. The Lord has delegated "manna" for each generation displaying perpetual depths of His greatness and truth. He is the very fountain of *all* wisdom and the source of *all* knowledge.

He expects His people who possess His Spirit to embrace every Word that He utters and the continual unfolding of biblical truth. In the Holy Place, the Table of Shewbread (bread of His presence) was a symbol of thanksgiving for His divine provision. After serving its purpose in the Holy Place it was consumed by the priests. We must consume every revelation of the Lord to be molded into His image and bear His attributes.

> Behold, I am about to build a house for the name of the LORD my God, dedicating it to Him, to burn fragrant incense before Him, and to set out *the show-bread continually*, and to offer burnt offerings morning and evening, on sabbaths and on new moons and on the appointed feasts of the LORD our God, this being required forever in Israel. And the house which I am about to build will be great; for greater is our God than all the gods. But who is able to build a house for Him, for the heavens and the highest heavens cannot contain Him? So who am I, that I should build a house for Him, except to burn incense before Him?
> —2 CHRONICLES 2:4–6 (EMPHASIS ADDED)

The Lord Jesus was the Word incarnate. To partake of Him

is to share in the revelation of God. The Word again desires to become flesh and live among us, doing the same works through us that He did while on the earth in human form.

Much has been written and spoken about the soon-emerging government of God. This is the governmental design in its purest form—Christ in us, the hope of glory. We then share in the mind of Christ providing an expression of His divine attributes, power and authority.

> **Jesus said to them, "I am the bread of life; he who comes to Me shall not hunger, and he who believes in Me shall never thirst."**
>
> **—JOHN 6:35**

The message for this hour is to be careful to receive the full revelation of Jesus Christ as revealed by the Holy Spirit through the Word of God. The light from the lampstand provides the illumination of the shewbread and the full revelation of God.

Paul once announced that he did not shun declaring the whole counsel of God in his preaching of the gospel. We need the "whole counsel" in order to be presented to the Lord Jesus and enter the Most Holy Place and union with God. To deny any portion of the sacred Scriptures is to embrace unbelief, the sin that kept the children of Israel from entering the Promised Land after their deliverance from Egypt.

In Him is the bread of life that He freely imparts to those who come to him unbridled and hungry for His presence. However, we cannot come to Him cloaked in worldly conformity but clothed in His righteousness, bearing His image and likeness. We are sanctified in truth, and His Word is truth. (See John 17:17.)

Abiding in the fear of the Lord

One of the Scriptures greatly emphasized for this season

conveys the seven eyes of God ranging to and fro throughout the earth. The "eyes" are represented by the golden lampstand and symbolic of the Lord's omniscience. To accomplish the destiny of the Church in our generation, we must be joined with Him, participating in divine insight and focusing our efforts according to the heavenly outline.

The seven Spirits of God standing before the throne features the full manifestation of the sevenfold Spirit of God resting in God's people. Where present, He produces the divine life and the revelation of God as portrayed in the ministry of Christ while He lived on the earth in human form.

To walk in the deep and intimate knowledge of Christ, we must also carry within us reverential awe of Him. These two spirits work in unison. The fear of the Lord is a corridor through which so many divine attributes are released through the Church and are essential to entering and maintaining His empowering presence.

Living understanding concerning the Lord's ways in heaven and on earth, birthed through the fear of the Lord, is the beginning of wisdom and knowledge and living. It is essential for the operation of the manifest presence of God in our lives in accordance with the nature and character displayed throughout the life of Christ.

We must come to understand the great significance of the fear of the Lord and our utter inability to produce it in the "soulish" realm of man. It is strictly an impartation from the divine nature worn as a mantle and resting upon those who have sought Him with their whole heart and have overcome the spirit of this world. Our fervent prayer should be for the "fear of the Lord" to rest in us in full measure.

Living in meekness

The fear of the Lord manifested in the spirit of a person will always produce meekness. Meekness is primarily being

teachable and willing to change when confronted with issues
contrary to the character of God. Meekness is by no means a
sign of weakness. It is simply the willingness to be molded
into the image of Christ. It is characterized in gentleness of
spirit and mildness of disposition.

> **Blessed are the meek [gentle, mild], for they shall
> inherit the earth.**
> —MATTHEW 5:5 (NKJV)

If we are to be yoked with the Lord in nature and purpose, we will come before the Father in the same manner
as the Lord: in gentleness (meekness) and humility. When we
are able to approach the throne of God in this posture,
we will begin to experience His manifest presence.

> **Take My yoke upon you, and learn from Me, for I
> am gentle and humble in heart; and you shall find
> rest for your souls.**
> —MATTHEW 11:29

When this takes place, we must overcome the great tendency to "do something" and merely remain still and reverential in His presence. This will produce a heart of admiration
and worship beyond anything we could ever imagine. There is
a time to be busy about the Lord's work and a time to be still
with our faces pressed to His feet in worship and adoration.

The illumination of the Holy Spirit in us will provide the
discernment between the two. Those who have experienced
His manifest presence can readily testify that the power of
such a presence will produce an awe and penetrating worship beyond the comprehension of man.

The "fear of the Lord" will awaken us to the time to be
"hushed" and sit in silent admiration. The Scriptures
admonish us to not grieve the Holy Spirit of God, whereby
we are sealed until the day of our redemption. Carelessness

and presumption clearly grieve the Holy Spirit. We must overcome these soulish tendencies if we are to enter into His glory and advance to even higher realms of glory.

> **But we all, with unveiled face beholding as in a mirror the glory of the Lord, are being transformed into the same image from glory to glory, just as from the Lord, the Spirit.**
>
> **—2 CORINTHIANS 3:18**

The Scriptures entreat us to go from glory to glory. A review of past outpourings of the Spirit will affirm that historically we have been unable to *maintain* the glory wondrously released to the Church. This failure has prevented us from moving into higher realms of glory. We must understand the divine principles that allow us to sustain the glory released so we can proceed further to the greater realms of glory He desires to display in us.

The Lord is aspiring to overshadow us to examine our innermost being and make changes that fashion us to be compatible with His Holy Spirit. In this process, if we will passionately call upon Him, He will release strength in our weaknesses to help change the areas we are unable to change on our own. This will allow us to return to the innocence of "babes," thus pleasing in the sight of the Father.

> **Truly I say to you, unless you are converted and become like children, you shall not enter the kingdom of heaven. Whoever then humbles himself as this child, he is the greatest in the kingdom of heaven.**
>
> **—MATTHEW 18:3–4**

A child is totally dependent upon his parents to provide care and protection. It is at this place of reliance that we begin to grow up and develop in His likeness.

Chapter 15

THE EXAMPLE
OF SAMUEL

GRACIOUSLY, THE LORD granted another very compelling prophetic experience or vision to depict the preparation necessary to fulfill our End-Time mandate. In it, a prophet we know and have utmost respect for, entered a room of leaders being prepared for the next season of the Spirit. The mature and loyal prophet stood before the leaders and announced with great power and strength, *"The apostolic is coming."* As he did, a voice of ultimate authority echoed from heaven, "The apostolic is coming."

With that affirmation, the prophet continued, "We had better get a good understanding of apostolic ministry under us . . . for it will be on top of us before we know it. Samuel is a type of this apostolic leadership. The Lord did let none of his words fall to the ground nor did he beg his bread from the people."

The spirit of prophecy

Through the experience, the Lord is indicating valuable attributes in the life and ministry of the prophet Samuel, depicting qualities He desires to impart to the apostolic leadership soon to emerge. Careful study of the life of Samuel will provide key secrets to help us qualify for this leadership and touch the heart of the Father in our preparation.

Very often, in prophetic experiences of this nature, a person we know and recognize as a true prophet of the Lord can actually represent the Lord Himself or the spirit of prophecy, bringing a timely message from the heart of God.

When the prophet announced on the earth that the apostolic was coming, it was verified with a heavenly voice to accentuate its certainty. In the Scriptures, when the Holy Spirit descended upon the Lord to assume residence in Him, a voice descended from heaven as an affirmation of this great reality. (See Luke 3:22.)

Likewise, when the disciples witnessed the Lord's transfiguration, they also heard the affirming Voice declaring Him to be the Son of God whose words were eternal. The attesting voice from heaven punctuates a truth that is established with certainty to be readily accepted.

The apostolic is coming, and the better understanding we have of it under us, the more capable we will be to sustain this awesome ministry without being overcome by the intensity and power of it. It must be our earnest prayer to faithfully administer this notable responsibility with character and integrity.

Saying only what He says

The Lord let none of Samuel's words fall to the ground. What a profound indication of intimacy and relationship between the Lord and His leadership.

> **So Samuel grew, and the LORD was with him and let none of his words fall to the ground.**
> —1 SAMUEL 3:19 (NKJV)

We are called to likewise be so intimate with the Lord that we say nothing in His name but what we have received by "a revelation of Jesus Christ." (See Galatians 1:12.)

Samuel did not speak in the name of the Lord presumptuously nor carelessly. Therefore, the Lord was able to perfectly support the words he spoke to the people as His spokesman.

The Scriptures describe the Lord, our ultimate example, as being so yielded to the Holy Spirit that He said nothing but what He heard from the Father and did nothing but what He saw the Father doing.

Do you not believe that I am in the Father, and the Father is in Me? The words that I say to you I do not speak on My own initiative, but the Father abiding in Me does His works.

—JOHN 14:10

We can likewise abide in a place of surrender to the Holy Spirit that He would let none of our words "fall to the ground" because we would not speak in His name unless we first heard from Him.

For all who are being led by the Spirit of God, these are sons of God.

—ROMANS 8:14

The Holy Spirit abiding in us will do the same works through us that He did in the Lord, fulfilling the prophetic promise of John 14:12.

He did not beg his bread from the people

One of the most notable attributes in the life of Samuel was his determination not to abuse his position and privileges before God and the people. There was not one person in all of Israel who could bear witness against Samuel, charging that he pleaded for money, possessions or property. Neither did he allow the spirit of this world to affect his ability to judge the people in righteousness and equity. The apostolic leadership soon to emerge should likewise be characterized by humility and genuine love for the people.

> I have walked before you from my youth even to this day. Here I am; bear witness against me before the LORD and His anointed. Whose ox have I taken, or whose donkey have I taken, or whom have I defrauded? Whom have I oppressed, or from whose hand have I taken a bribe to blind my eyes with it? I will restore it to you. And they said, "You have not defrauded us, or oppressed us, or taken anything from any man's hand."
>
> —1 SAMUEL 12:2-4

The apostle Paul admonished the church of Corinth and the Church of this day to stand in righteousness and to judge the affairs of men with wisdom and truth. To do so we must possess the character of Christ reflected in Samuel and be free from the tendency to abuse the anointing and authority of God for unrighteous gain.

Certainly, there is a place for giving and supporting the work of the ministry and sharing in the fruitful labors of the anointing. This is an issue of the heart, and like Paul, we must pray to be trustworthy stewards of the mysteries, power and provisions of God.

The prosperity coming to the Church will be for kingdom purposes, not for personal luxury or extravagance. The apostolic church in the Book of Acts shared all things in common and delegated resources according to need, reflecting love and unity.

The Lord's spokesman

Like Samuel, the anointed leadership the Lord desires to bring to His Church will stand before Him as His spokesmen, extracting the precious from the profane. To them, the Lord will be as a fortified wall of bronze, and though the enemy will contend with them, he will not prevail because the Lord will be present to save and deliver. This will further the restoration promised through the prophet Joel.

The ministry of Samuel was established by the Lord's manifest presence in the order of Moses and Aaron. As priests, they were charged with the role of intercession on behalf of God's people and instruction in the ways of righteousness. Faithfulness in these areas will begin to lead the Church out of "Babylonian" confusion and restore her to a place of loyalty and consecration to the Lord. If the Lord can find a people without *mixture* He will send the Spirit without *measure*.

> Moses and Aaron were among His priests, and Samuel was among those who called on His name; they called upon the Lord, and He answered them. He spoke to them in the pillar of cloud; they kept His testimonies and the statute that He gave them.
> —PSALM 99:6–7

These faithful leaders were transitional men in covenant relationship with the Lord for transitional times and marked a point of demarcation for the people of God. This perfectly illustrates the nature of the apostolic leadership the Lord will use in this day.

These three men represent the priest-prophet-judge (kingly) anointing that will be entrusted to maturing leadership. To each of these three, God proved Himself in mercy and in judgment.

Standing before the Lord

Moses was one of the Lord's foremost representatives, standing before Him as His spokesman in a position of righteousness displaying the Father's pure judgments. Moses was able to occupy this distinguished position of great honor and responsibility because of the prior years of preparation, purging and refinement that qualified him.

Each of these men already possessed a deposit of His virtue, yet the testing of their righteousness produced a multiplied measure of divine character enabling them to accomplish the high calling of God for their generation.

Amos is another example of one called by the Spirit to foresee the judgment of God and stand before His presence and intercede on behalf of His people.

> Thus the Lord GOD showed me: Behold, He formed locust swarms at the beginning of the late crop; indeed it was the late crop after the king's mowings. And so it was, when they had finished eating the grass of the land, that I said: "O Lord GOD, forgive, I pray! Oh, that Jacob may stand, for he is small!" So the LORD relented concerning this. "It shall not be," said the LORD.
>
> —AMOS 7:13 (NKJV)

The Lord has identified those who occupy this unique position as "His friends." What an incredible honor to be called the friend of God and a great responsibility that accompanies this commission of intercession and leadership.

Daniel was described in the Scriptures as one greatly beloved because, at least in part, of his heart for the nation and his willingness to stand in the gap for his people. He humbled himself and presented supplications on behalf of God's people through a heart of repentance and foresight for the seasons ahead.

The Lord's "friends" are able to stand in this post because of the enlightenment they possess through affectionate exchange with the Lord that enables them to occupy this privileged place in God. Intimate fellowship results from the testing of righteousness allowing one to peer into the very heart of God to obtain understanding of His nature and character. In this manner, divine purposes are birthed in the earth through words anointed with spirit and life expressed from this position of righteousness.

The Lord our mediator

Principally, the Lord is looking for a righteous agent on the earth to stand in the gap on behalf of a sinful generation and represent Him and the revelation of His kingdom. The Lord Himself is the perfect mediator between God and man establishing for all generations the righteousness of God. That virtue is now being imparted to those in the Church established in fidelity as His delegates in the earth standing in the gap on behalf of this evil generation.

> **But now He has obtained a more excellent ministry, inasmuch as He is also Mediator of a better covenant, which was established on better promises.**
> **—HEBREWS 8:6**

An increased emphasis on power evangelism worldwide will increase as the intervention of heaven is unleashed through intercessory prayer. Power evangelism is the appearance of heavenly power drawing the people to the cross by the demonstration of the Spirit. As meetings are held and manifestations of His glory emerge, sinners will come to the altar for salvation and deliverance. We will begin to see the infancy of this now, but it will increase as the Church matures.

The Father has chosen the Church as His instrument to unfold His great redemptive plan. To fulfill our highest purpose, we too must discover that cherished and honorable position as "the Lord's friends." When thus seated with Christ in the heavenlies, we become an expression of His intercessory role, calling upon the Father for mercy in the midst of judgment. When this is achieved, we have the Lord's promise for restoration and salvation for man.

> **If there is a messenger for him, a mediator, one among a thousand, to show man His uprightness, Then He is gracious to him, and says, "Deliver him from going down to the Pit; I have found a ransom."**
> **—JOB 33:23–24 (NKJV)**

Those with the unique distinction as "friends" are the ones who have come to possess His traits and holy qualities. It is the responsibility of the Lord's "friends" to remind Him of His sure promises to each generation and stay His hand of judgment that the whole earth may be filled with the knowledge of His glory.

It is always the enemy's desire to boast that the Lord was able to bring the people out but not carry them in. The Lord's "friends" continually petition the throne of grace with the promises of God and the expression of His divine attributes of lovingkindness and mercy.

The "friends" of God will occupy an important place of intercession on behalf of the people, not because of any excellence of their own but because of His great compassion. From this position of favor, we are allowed to intercede for others by calling upon the grace of God to grant a heart of divine repentance, leading to the knowledge of the truth and escaping the snare of the devil having been held captive by him to do his will.

Priest-prophet-judge anointing

The coming apostolic ministers will be as pillar of cloud by day with prophetic anointing that will function as a pillar of fire by night giving illumination. Each will provide a canopy of protection through the Holy Spirit in the same way Israel was protected during the judgments of Egypt. The shelter of "Goshen" will become apparent in the coming season.

The Lord will allow nothing to come upon the earth unless He first reveals His secret counsel to His servants. (See Amos 3:7.) Moses, Aaron and Samuel each represent types of the coming government. The manner in which the Lord used these men will also portray the coming leadership and God's dealings with them. He is going to give divinely granted understanding.

The Scriptures declare that the breath of God gives understanding. He is going to breathe upon us to give comprehension of these times and the things we must do to walk intimately with Him as His habitation.

Commissioning and release

Even though Samuel was born through covenant relationship with incredible destiny, he did not experience the supernatural dealings of God until his prophetic commissioning.

> Now Samuel did not yet know the LORD, nor had the word of the LORD yet been revealed to him.
> —1 SAMUEL 3:7

There may be many who feel as though they do not qualify for this type of leadership because they have not had prophetic or supernatural experiences in their life. However, the Scriptures make it plain: the Word of the Lord had not appeared to Samuel until a very specific commissioning experience released him into his purpose and calling.

Many of today's "Samuel-type" leaders have been hidden and unfamiliar with the visions and revelations of the Lord. Nonetheless, great and profound expressions of the Spirit are imminently awaiting these leaders once the grooming is complete and the timing appropriate for their release.

Chapter 16

FROM THE DUNGEON TO THE THRONE

IMMEDIATELY PRIOR TO the Day of Atonement 2001, the Lord granted another dream continuing His teaching of the soon emerging apostolic ministry. During this experience, I witnessed and participated in a battle that was taking place between the army of light and the army of darkness.

In a way that can only be expressed in symbolic experiences of this nature, it seemed the score was being kept between the two armies as the conflict heightened. At some points the army of darkness was pressing the army of light and the score would reflect that advance in much the same way that a sporting event would keep score.

Then, the army of light would rally and begin to take ground against the army of darkness, and the scoreboard would likewise change to show the army of light in the lead. This transition took place many times with the lead changing hands on numerous occasions until time was about to expire on the clock.

With only seconds remaining in the contest, the army of darkness was leading on the scoreboard and rallied all their strength for one last assault in their attempt to totally overrun the army of light. As we in the army of light observed the scoreboard and discovered only seconds remaining, we called upon the Lord with all our strength. In an unprecedented release of divine grace, He intervened on our behalf, allowing us to mount a formidable assault, achieving a great victory as "time" ran out.

The victory was significant and the jubilant celebration erupted among those participating in the army of light. As we were enjoying the Lord's great grace and the victory He had given, I looked at the scoreboard. To my surprise the score read, 41–41. Needless to say, I was somewhat dismayed at this discovery.

The victory was sure, and the celebration was evident; I knew it was not a tie. A voice then spoke and said, "Genesis 41:41." I understood this parable could be interpreted from the truth communicated in Genesis 41:41, although at the time I was uncertain of the specific wording of this passage.

> **And Pharaoh said to Joseph, "See I have set you over all the land of Egypt." Then Pharaoh took off his signet ring from his hand, and put it on Joseph's hand, and clothed him in garments of fine linen, and put the gold necklace around his neck.**
> —GENESIS 41:41–42

As I began to meditate upon this notable Scripture and the promotion of Joseph from the dungeon to the throne in a single day, the Lord began to quicken significant truth related to our calling as the apostolic Church. The dream related that we had received the grace to overcome the resistance of the enemy that attempts to prohibit the birthing of this significant ministry designated for the End-Time.

I had never before recognized the often promised "Joseph" anointing was much more than providing a great source of plenty in time of famine. Included in this significant calling and commission is an apostolic mantle with bold spiritual authority and Godly character.

Threefold "Joseph" anointing

The emerging "Joseph" ministry will be much more than providing a source of plenty in time of deficiency. The true Joseph ministry is a threefold anointing as typified in Genesis 41:42.

> **Then Pharaoh took off his signet ring from his hand, and put it on Joseph's hand, and clothed him in garments of fine linen, and put the gold necklace around his neck.**
>
> **—Genesis 41:42**

In one day Joseph was elevated from the dungeon to the throne. Joseph received first the signet ring illustrating the spiritual authority that will emerge in the "Joseph" company. The ring of authority was given to announce to all that Joseph had the full influence of the king and answered only to the king in his power.

Secondly, Joseph was also dressed in linen garments to prophetically depict the priesthood of the Lord, clothed in purity and the nature of Christ. This prominent ministry will require great meekness of heart because of the natural and spiritual resources that will be confided in them.

Finally, Joseph received a gold chain to exemplify the prosperity that will be entrusted to this company. The purposes of God will require great sums of resources to fully accomplish End-Time ministry and fulfill the will of God in the earth. These will include places of refuge and provision for those who will be persecuted as well as those displaced by the extreme natural disasters and military confrontations that will be taking place.

Overcoming the devourer

Facilitating the revelation of the kingdom throughout the earth, along with historic circumstances about to take place worldwide, will require considerable resources devoted for this purpose. Part of the promise for our day is the emerging "Joseph" ministries that will provide a great source of plenty in time of famine.

The enemy knows that day is imminent and is assigning weighty demonic assaults against the financial structure of individuals and the overall economy of our country. His primary aim is to deplete resources to hinder our ability to invest in divine opportunities.

It is not presently the desire of the Lord for our economy to be destroyed, although recent events have been allowed in order to awaken us to the seriousness of the hour. With that assurance, we can pray with greater authority and power against the demonic forces devouring our financial resources individually and within the Church.

This awareness can radically change our entire perspective of prayer when we recognize the enemy assault against our economy and the emerging "Joseph" ministries. That is another of the many reasons for the arising of intercessory ministries in the order of Esther who pave the way for the righteous government typified by Mordecai.

It is the power of the enemy, and we must take our stand and ask the Lord to rebuke the devourer on our behalf and open the windows of heaven to release His blessings upon the pure-hearted to become a source of plenty. Even so, we must be careful not to place our faith and confidence in the economy but only in the Lord's ability to use us and the blessings He provides to facilitate the revelation of His kingdom.

Emerging champions

Satan is planning a major assault against the Church financially. He plans to attempt to deplete our resources to frustrate our ability to support the great move of God coming to the earth and hinder our reinforcement of Israel. This can be overcome through prayer and the awakening of the Church to her apostolic destiny. There are many men and women hidden in recent years being groomed by the Holy Spirit to meet the challenges and needs of this generation.

A careful study and examination of both biblical and natural history will support the conclusion that God creates men and women to meet the challenges and needs of the generation to which they are born. This can readily be recognized in Scripture with the emergence of prominent prophets, judges and leaders who led Israel during times of apostasy, adversity, prosperity and war.

In modern history, we can evaluate World War II and discover the advent of distinguished leaders, such as George Patton and Douglas MacArthur. These great commanders acknowledged that their earliest memories consisted of becoming military leaders and fulfilling their destiny as conquerors.

From the time of their youth, each devoted himself to the preparation, training and strategy necessary to be regarded among the greatest military leaders in modern history. Clearly, the Lord imparted this desire in them at an early age in order to meet the distresses of our nation and the free world during the great conflict of World War II.

A generation of destiny

The Lord is also creating and preparing a body of spiritual warriors to emerge in our generation to meet the spiritual challenges and prophetic destiny ordained for our age and foretold in Scripture. One of the greatest mandates of all time is to cooperate with the Holy Spirit to taste the good Word of God and the power of the age to come and see the biblical directive in Numbers 14:21 fulfilled—to be the instruments by which He fills the whole earth with His glory.

> So the LORD said, "I have pardoned them according to your word; but indeed, as I live, all the earth will be filled with the glory of the Lord."
> —NUMBERS 14:20–21

Like Abraham, it is the cry of our hearts, "My lord, if now I have found favor in your sight, please do not pass your servant by" (Genesis 18:3). It should be our earnest desire and aspiration to be the chosen generation through which the Lord will give revelation and expression of His nature, character and power that we may begin to fill the entire earth with the glory of God. That would be the fulfillment of the awesome prayer outlined by the Lord Himself, "Thy Kingdom come. Thy will be done, on earth as it is in heaven" (Matthew 6:10).

We have the incredible privilege of living in the generation that will witness the unveiling of great mysteries and hidden secrets reserved for the time of the end. (See Daniel 12:4.) Thankfully, the Holy Spirit is beginning to unleash "great and mighty" things related to our prophetic mandate from the Scriptures and imparting insight with understanding concerning the revelation of His glory.

With perfect certainty, there will be a company of people who reside in this place of promise. Just as surely as the prophetic fulfillment of the restoration of the Jewish people to the land of Israel miraculously took place, so also will there be the divinely motivated establishment of the Bride to her inheritance.

In the same way we witnessed the awakening of the Jewish people to their homeland, so will the Bride be awakened to her birthright. There will initially be a message of restoration for those with ears to hear, followed by times of intense tribulation and difficulty that will drive the people to the fulfillment of God's Word.

Fishers and hunters

Early one morning just as the sun was rising, I heard a voice in a dream saying, "I am going to send both the fishers and the hunters." Naturally, I initially related this pointed statement to the restoration of the Jewish people to their native land and the establishment of a sovereign state. I later discovered a broader application of this certainty.

One of the most profound prophetic accomplishments in human history is the restoration of the Jewish people following the diaspora. Never before has a nation been dead for almost 20 centuries and then reborn in accordance with prophecies recorded over 2,500 years ago. Even so, our generation has witnessed this astounding fact, and we recognize that only God's sovereign power could accomplish such a miraculous undertaking. God's Word cannot fail. Every "jot and tittle" will be accomplished in its entirety.

> "'As the LORD lives, who brought up the sons of Israel from the land of the north and from all the countries where He had banished them.' For I will restore them to their own land which I gave to their fathers. Behold, I am going to send for many fishermen," declares the LORD, "and they will fish for them; and afterwards I shall send for many hunters, and they will hunt them from every mountain and every hill, and from the clefts of the rocks."
> —JEREMIAH 16:15–16

Jeremiah prophesied the manner in which the Lord would execute this notable task after many centuries of dispersion, persecution and murder. He foresaw that the Lord would birth in the hearts of men the vision of restoration of a natural homeland and entice the Jewish people to return to their inheritance. They were the "fishers" who delivered a message of restoration and promise.

Among them were great leaders such as Theodore Herzl, recognized as the founder of modern Zionism who laid the foundation for the creation of sovereign rule in 1896 through his book, *The Jewish State.* Another was Chaim Weizman, the first president of the Jewish state and creator of the World Zionist Organization, aimed at encouraging Jews worldwide to help develop and settle Israel. The Hebrew language was reintroduced under the leadership of Eliezer Ben-Jehudah and others.

As is generally the case when the Lord births something new, the restorers' views were met with mixed reactions among the Jewish community. Nehemiah also encountered similar opposition in his commission for the reestablishment of the Temple. In spite of the resistance and difficulties, there would be a people who returned and fulfilled this biblical mandate.

Their message awakened in the hearts of many Jewish people the desire to return to their own land. Many were willing to forsake the wealth, friendships and security of the nations in which they were sojourning to return to their heritage. The early pioneers laid the foundation for the economic and social rebirth of the Jewish nation. They paved the way for the Lord's timing when conditions were ripe to possess the land promised to Abraham and his seed.

"Also I will restore the captivity of My people Israel, and they will rebuild the ruined cities and live in

them, they will also plant vineyards and drink their wine, and make gardens and eat their fruit. I will also plant them on their land, and they will not again be rooted out from their land which I have given them," says the Lord your God.

—Amos 9:14–15

"Zionism" became a rallying cry for the Jewish people, and many from Europe and Russia answered the call, provoked by the proud beliefs of the movement. It proved to be an awakening in many for rebuilding the country. During the years 1882–1905 more than 25,000 Jews, mostly from Eastern Europe, arrived in the land of Palestine. Between 1905 and the outbreak of WWI another 40,000 immigrated.[1]

Following the "fishers," another form of motivation began to emerge in the form of the "hunters." The intense persecution and anti-Semitism prevailing throughout Europe and especially Russia during the late nineteenth and early twentieth centuries, began to hasten the development of modern Zionism. Finally, the genocide of Hitler's insanity forged another exodus, driving the Jewish people to the creation of a state and their independence.

God used these persecutions to press the Jewish masses home, although it was Satan's brash intent to completely eradicate worldwide Jewry and circumvent the ultimate plan of God. As it turned out, because of the atrocities of the Holocaust, the horrified nations of the world granted official sanctions for a Jewish state, and on May 14, 1948 Israel was born. Over the following three decades almost two million Jews would return to their homeland. Naturally, the numbers have increased substantially since then.

Our fishers and hunters

It is an interesting observation to note that in 1896 when Theodore Herzl published his book *The Jewish State*, arousing the Jewish people to the restoration of their inheritance, Alexander Dowie was also in Zion, Illinois, commissioning an apostolic ministry and awakening the Church to the restoration of her inheritance. Likewise, in 1948 with the official recognition of the Jewish state, the Church was also experiencing the Healing Revival. It is clear there is an undeniable link between Israel and the Church.

At the same time the Lord was restoring the land of Israel, and eventually Jerusalem, into the hands of the Jewish people, He was also awakening spiritual Israel to her inheritance. In the same manner that the Jewish people were dispersed among the nations of the earth, so also were Spirit-filled Christians scattered among the many religious institutions and organizations following the compromise of Nicaea in A.D. 325.

Israel realized her prophetic fulfillment with the establishment of a sovereign state. Likewise, the Bride residing in her full inheritance must also be apprehended. Heaven will retain the Lord Jesus until that covenant declaration is accomplished. As with Israel, there will be the perfect accomplishment of God's Word relative to the Bride of Christ who has been betrothed to Him and will know His intimate chambers.

Our spiritual Promised Land is in view, and God's mandate will be accomplished. He will first utilize the "fishers" to entice and lure many to the spiritual domain of our inheritance and fruitfulness with a prophetic message of restoration. He will then allow the "hunters" to drive still others from necessity to the place of promise. There will be an overcoming Body who will occupy their birthright. The

Scriptures declare it to be so.

The Lord has always had His faithful remnant throughout Church history that modeled their faith according to the standards established by the early Church. Numerous End-Time prophecies within the Scriptures will become timely as the Church is fashioned according to His design. The full stature of the apostolic Church will be functioning in our day, shaping a "called-out" body of believers to function in kingdom power and authority.

The time of the end is a period for revealing and reinstating truth and exposing the hidden things of darkness. "Restorers" are beginning to emerge with a "fisher" anointing, birthing desire in the hearts of Christians for the full measure of God regardless of the opposition.

> But all things that are exposed are made manifest by the light, for whatever makes manifest is light. Therefore He says: "Awake, you who sleep, arise from the dead, and Christ will give you light." See then that you walk circumspectly, not as fools but as wise, redeeming the time, because the days are evil.
>   —EPHESIANS 5:13–16 (NKJV)

The rebuilding of our apostolic heritage can be achieved through desperate hearts pursuing the Lord and the fullness of His heritage awakened through the "fishers." It can also be experienced through persecution, or God's discipline on "spiritual Babylon," driving His covenant people to the land of their promise by the "hunters."

The Lord has pledged to reverse the captivity of His people and be jealous for His holy name. At that time we will forget the shame and reproach of our unfaithfulness and begin to dwell securely in the land of our promise. Through His justice and holiness He will set apart and vindicate His people from the hand of their enemies. This is true both for natural and spiritual Israel.

It is our prayer that each will receive with hearing ears and sincere hearts the message of the "fishers" and respond to the call to enter our destiny. It will behoove us to notice the example of the Jewish people according to the admonition of the apostle Paul for therein we discover God's ways.

PART VII

TOKENS OF APOSTOLIC AND KINGDOM REALITY

Chapter 17

KINGDOM PRINCIPLES

WHEN I FIRST received the baptism of the Spirit in 1989, the Lord thankfully imparted an insatiable hunger to understand His anointing and a yearning to study the lives of men and women who walked closely with Him. During those years, I would purchase every book I could locate that addressed the anointing of revelation and power carried to the people by men and women of faith. This included listening to hundreds of audio- and videotapes shared by the leaders who possessed an understanding of the Spirit and His power.

Throughout this process the Lord began to demonstrate how He had given "tokens" of kingdom reality that would characterize the End-Time generation. These "tokens" were men and women who pressed in to the Lord and seemingly stood head and shoulders above others and touched something that transcended their generation. It was as though they were born out of season.

They certainly carried gifts of the Spirit described in 1 Corinthians 12 but also reached over into the kingdom age and began to "taste the good word of God and the power of the age to come." They became a "prototype" of an entire company of people who will characterize the time of the end, men and women, such as Maria Woodworth-Etter,

John G. Lake, William Branham and Alexander Dowie.
Careful study of their lives will glean key insights into the
heart of the Father and uncover golden nuggets of great value
that will assist us in attaining that place with the Lord. We
can also discern mistakes that were made and pray for the
grace and understanding not to make them ourselves. The
enemy will continue to utilize plots and schemes formerly
successful in his attempt to derail God's anointed vessels.

It was by researching and analyzing God's anointed
"friends" that various messages began to emerge concerning
the soul of man and the superior value in the thorough
redemption of our mind, will and emotions by the compre-
hensive surrender of every department of our lives. I
observed how this reality was a common denominator consistently apparent in each, allowing a greater dimension of
intimacy and fellowship with the Lord.

When the veils of our soul are removed, we begin to
behold Him with an unveiled face and reflect His image and
nature. Only in that place can we faithfully carry the powerful anointing of revelation and power essential for our
mandate and commission.

Tokens of kingdom ministry

Throughout Church history, the many expressions of
revival and outpouring have provided numerous saints who
genuinely knew God and yielded examples of true apostolic
ministry. These individuals attained a mature stature, quali-
fying them as a dwelling place for the Spirit of God through
which the Lord was able to function and do His works.
They were men and women so thoroughly filled with the
Holy Spirit that they exercised the Lord's dominion over
demons, disease and death.

These saints were radical gestures of the life of Christ
with His divine nature radiating through them, men and

women who were crucified with Christ living by the faith of the Son of God.

I do not believe it is because the Lord's love for these individuals was greater; it seems they were willing to pay a price that allowed for a deeper walk with Him. The Holy Spirit has clearly demonstrated His intent to have a company of people through this generation who will know their God and do mighty exploits on His behalf. They will be transparent vessels whose only desire is friendship with God.

Tremendous lessons can be extracted by examining the lives of these spiritual champions to determine the secrets to their success with God and also learn from the mistakes that would sometimes entangle them.

Remember the days of old, consider the years of all generations. Ask your father, and he will inform you, your elders, and they will tell you.
—DEUTERONOMY 32:7

"Remember the days of old" and consider the generations of long ago. The admonition, given to Israel through Moses, required the children of Israel to examine their past and gain understanding about the Lord's ways.

The same counsel has even greater value today as we challenge ourselves to understand our Christian heritage and learn about God's dealings with man and His sovereign ways. By studying the generations of long ago we discover heavenly blueprints for our day. While we do not want to live in the past, we can examine the past and extract nuggets of wisdom concerning God's ways and also learn from the miscalculations of our Christian Fathers.

Back to our future

Since the days of Martin Luther and the early Reformation, the Lord has continually demonstrated a progressive restoration of truth and power through the revelation of Himself to the Church. This unveiling and re-introduction of our inheritance has been line upon line and precept upon precept, continually unfolding fresh disclosure of Himself and His Word.

This process is for the purpose of restoring the Church to her former apostolic authority as realized in the first century Church and the walk of intimacy and friendship with the Lord that was enjoyed by the early disciples. Once we experience this full restoration, we are then equipped and conditioned for the even higher destiny prophetically foretold and symbolized through the biblical Feast of Tabernacles.

As we consider the prior generations and the tokens of lives devoted to the Lord, we can relish the revelation given to them and also learn from the mistakes. As the Scriptures point out, the scribe who becomes a disciple of the kingdom is like the head of a household who brings forth from his treasure, both things old and new. (See Matthew 13:52.)

True apostolic ministry

Apostolic ministry can be defined as Jesus Christ manifested and abiding in His Church, doing the same works through His Church that He did while living on the earth in human form. True kingdom ministry is a fulfillment of John 14:12, the Holy Spirit performing the same works through the Church that He did through the life and ministry of the Lord Jesus Christ.

There is a ministry of perfection that is to come to the Church that will ultimately prepare her for the return of the Bridegroom. However, before we can begin to move toward the ministry of perfection, we must first return to our future. We must realize the complete restoration of biblical apostolic ministry of calling out and separating the Church from the world to prepare her in excellence for the bridegroom.

In Joel 2:25 the Lord makes a wonderful promise to restore all that the palmerworm, cankerworm, caterpillar and the locust have destroyed. These four stages of a maturing locust are used to prophetically symbolize the way the spirit of antichrist would attack the Lord's Church in its attempt to steal our birthright and the gospel of salvation and power. Nonetheless, the Lord Himself foretold the Spirit of Elijah being released to a generation to "restore all things." (See Matthew 17:11.)

The early apostolic Church is typified as a tree the Lord planted and nurtured to full maturity, bearing divine fruit. The spirit of antichrist is symbolized by the locust devouring first the fruit, then the leaves, the bark and finally gnawing into the very heart of the tree in order to destroy it. This final stage culminated in the era known as the Dark Ages.

The Lord's promise to restore began through the ministry of Martin Luther and has now matured to a level where this generation can expect the complete restoration of biblical apostolic ministry. This is our quest to return back to the future.

When our Lord was on the earth He chose the twelve He would groom and prepare for the birth of His Church. For three and one-half years, He planted the seed of the Word of God within their hearts, though very often without their full understanding of His instruction. When the Day of Pentecost had fully come, the Holy Spirit descended upon them and watered the seed within their hearts, producing the life of Christ and the revelation of His kingdom in the earth. This same process must be realized in this generation as well.

One of God's "tokens" is John G. Lake, and the following pages highlight significant truth in his life that is helpful in understanding our call to see the full restoration of the apostolic Church and demonstrate the kingdom design. His life illustrates one who lived the reality of the things outlined for our day and provided an example of one who "overcame."

Chapter 18

JOHN G. LAKE— AN APOSTLE OF FAITH

JOHN G. LAKE was a man who experienced apostolic ministry according to first-century standards and changed the world every place that he went. His life and ministry was a representation of a vessel yielded to God as a habitation for His manifest presence. Through him the Holy Spirit was able to heal the sick, cast out demons, save the lost, and manifest the very nature and character of Christ. He demonstrated that Jesus Christ is the same yesterday, today and forever.

By every biblical definition, the life of John G. Lake represented true apostolic ministry. Through him the great commission became reality and the kingdom of God was manifested on the earth. Great lessons can be learned from his life, revealing the keys to his power with God. Careful examination of his life and ministry can help the Church for the coming visitation and restoration.

Having the Lord's potential

When the time came for the Lord to be glorified through the sacrificial offering of His life, He made it clear that His life was likened unto a grain of wheat. When this grain of wheat dies it is for the purpose of bringing forth multiplied grains of wheat *like the original grain.*

> Most assuredly, I say to you, unless a grain of wheat falls into the ground and dies, it remains alone; but if it dies, it produces much grain.
>
> —JOHN 12:24 (NKJV)

The Bible teaches that when the Lord returns we are to be like Him. The Holy Spirit residing in us will reveal the same attributes through us as He did in the Lord Jesus Christ. This belief formed the cornerstone for the life and ministry of John G. Lake.

Lake believed the Lord would not commission us to do the works He did without adequately equipping us to do those works. He once commented, "We need to set our sights high and refuse the traditions of men who say that it is impossible to do as Jesus instructed us."[1]

True apostolic ministry is simply the extension of the ministry begun by the Lord, our ultimate example. The power of redemption is so great that sinners saved by grace and filled with the Holy Spirit are given the opportunity of carrying on the very ministry of Christ, doing the works He did. Lake is a token of this reality given to the twenty-first century. Our sights should be set equally as high.

His definition of the apostolic church

During the years preceding and following the turn of the twentieth century, Lake made a very notable and revealing observation. During those years there had been a tremendous outpouring of the Holy Spirit with great manifestations of power, signs and wonders. Their generation realized they were given an extraordinary opportunity of seeing the return of genuine apostolic ministry through the revelation of His kingdom.

Lake later discerned that his generation had missed the mark by not realizing the true definition of the Apostolic

Church. Some attempted to build an apostolic ministry around the doctrine and manifestation of healing power. Others aspired to establish the apostolic Church around the restoration of the gifts and speaking in tongues. Others endeavored to create and establish the apostolic order around the doctrine of holiness.

All of these qualities are attributes of the Holy Spirit and are essential to the Church, yet do not singularly sustain apostolic ministry. Lake observed that the people were absorbed in the phenomena of God and not the Person of God.

According to Lake, the truest definition of the apostolic Church can be expressed in the awesome and reverential experience of union with God and becoming One with Him. He believed the Church of his day did not regard the fullness of the Holy Spirit with the reverence due an experience so sacred and so terribly costly.

For this gift the Lord lived in the world, bled on the cross, entered the darkness of death, hell and the grave, grappled with and strangled the accursed powers of darkness, came forth again and finally ascended to heaven in order to secure it for His Church.

He believed apostolic ministry is defined and realized through individuals becoming the habitation of God—the Holy Spirit literally manifested in the spirit, soul and body of the believers, taking total possession of His Church, bestowing upon her His qualities, attributes and potential. This process was not merely a reformation; it was a renewal and a transformation. Men and women renewed by the Spirit of God and transformed by the Holy Spirit became one spirit with Him.

Union with the Holy Spirit was not merely a gift of power but of God Himself. Out of necessity, Lake became acquainted with the healing power of God through the ministry of Alexander Dowie. During the later years of the nineteenth century he was miraculously healed of terminal illness along with his brother, his sister and his wife. In addition, another sister was literally raised from the dead through the ministry of Dowie.

This introduction to the power of God began a quest in him not only to know the healing of God, but also the God of healing. His desire was fulfilled, he described, when he became the habitation of God in a powerful encounter with the Lord and His glory.

His experience

At the age of sixteen John G. Lake came to know the saving power of Christ. His salvation experience was a very real one, as displayed in his changed life. Many around him observed this transformation and said, "You are baptized in the Holy Ghost."

While friends around him were saying he had been filled with the Holy Spirit, Lake experienced a hunger for more of God that was almost unbearable. He began to pursue the Lord and came to know the sanctifying power of the Holy Spirit through the ministry of a layman named Melvin Pratt.

This precious brother introduced Lake to the washing of the water by the Word, producing in him a much richer and anointed life. Those around him acknowledged that surely he had received the baptism of the Holy Spirit. Yet Brother Lake hungered for more.

Several years later, Lake was introduced to the healing power of God through Alexander Dowie. After experiencing firsthand this great power, he moved to Zion, Illinois, and associated himself with Dowie. He received from the Holy Spirit a tremendous impartation of the healing anointing of God. Many miracles and manifestations of the Spirit followed him. Those around him again tried to convince him he had received the baptism of the Holy Spirit.

By the turn of the century Lake had realized a powerful salvation experience, an even more powerful sanctification encounter and an impartation of the ministry of healing. At each juncture, those around him tried to convince him he had received the fullness of the Holy Spirit, yet his heart burned for more of God than ever before.

As a result he began a season of fasting, praying and waiting upon the Lord for a nine-month duration. During this time he desperately searched for the place in God that would satisfy the longing of his heart. At the end of the time of separation, Lake had an awesome experience with the Lord. In it, Lake found himself surrounded in a cloud of glory. Volumes of virtue and power surged through his innermost being with waves of glory.

Lake later spoke of this experience saying, "The glory of this experience remained in my soul. I found that my life began to manifest in the varied range of the gifts of the Spirit. Healings were of a more powerful order. My nature became so sensitized that I could lay my hands on any man or woman and tell what organ was diseased, and to what extent."[2]

He knew he had been immersed in the Holy Spirit and had become a dwelling place of God. His heart and soul were now satisfied that the Holy Spirit was residing in him, speaking through him, and saturating every fiber of his being.

It was during this season that science even testified to the healing and re-creative power of the Holy Spirit. Lake would visit hospitals and begin to diagnose cases the doctors were unable to analyze. The physicians later testified his diagnoses were correct.

On another occasion he submitted himself to the scrutiny of microscopes and x-ray machines so doctors could witness the power of God as he prayed for individuals. They would actually attach the instruments to patients and watch through the most powerful instruments of science as tissue began to be restored and human cells responded to the power of prayer.

Finally his heart was satisfied that he had received the fullness of the Holy Spirit, producing the nature and character of Christ within him. He believed, as the Scriptures teach, this indwelling experience now equipped him to carry on the ministry of Christ as did the early apostles.

Triune salvation

During the winter of 1913, Lake presented a teaching to the Church of England entitled, "Triune Salvation." This teaching revealed a key secret to his power and intimacy with God.

So significant was its content that the Bishop of London wrote of it saying, "It contains the spirit of primitive Christianity and reveals the distinction between the Christian soul of the first and twentieth century, the Spirit of Christ's domain, by which Christianity attained its spiritual supremacy. It is one of the greatest sermons I have ever heard, and I recommend its careful study by every priest."[3]

In this study, Lake reveals the important significance of our complete redemption on all three levels of human life. Complete redemption of our spirit, perfect deliverance of our soul (mind), and complete freedom of our body.

> Now may the God of peace Himself sanctify you entirely; and may your spirit and soul and body be preserved complete, without blame at the coming of our Lord Jesus Christ.
>
> —1 THESSALONIANS 5:23

Lake taught that it was the tendency of the average Christian to cease in their quest for God at the atonement of their spirit. He believed it was equally as important for the believer to allow the Holy Spirit to sanctify the soul and the body in order for the individual to become the habitation of God.

The sanctification of the soul literally involved the impartation of the mind of Christ. John Wesley defined sanctification as "possessing the mind of Christ and all the mind of Christ."[4] This level of consecration was essential for our thoughts to be perfectly in tune with the Lord's thoughts and our ways consistent with His.

Complete sanctification of our soul and mind also involved the renewal of our emotions. Many believers are trapped in the tyranny of grief over the past. We are a new creation, and all things have become fresh; past failures have been erased by the blood of Christ.

Grief will ultimately lead to bitterness, and bitterness will defile. Consequently, it is essential that we allow the Holy Spirit to thoroughly consecrate and sanctify our soul, mind and emotions in order to become the tabernacle of the Holy Spirit.

Complete triune salvation also involved the separation of the believer from all that would defile, recognizing that our body is the temple of the Holy Spirit and should be consecrated accordingly. Romans 8:11 declares:

But if the Spirit of Him who raised Jesus from the dead dwells in you, He who raised Christ Jesus from the dead will also give life to your mortal bodies through His Spirit who indwells you.

The Lord's imparted life granted through the indwelling presence of the Holy Spirit will provide divine health and freedom from the lusts that are the result of man's fallen condition.

Lake taught that the genuine Christian is a separated person. Alienated forever unto God in all the departments of life; his body, his soul and his spirit are forever committed to the Lord. This absolute abandonment to God in "triune salvation" is the real secret to the successful Christian life and is essential to becoming the habitation of God.

Unconditional consecration makes the Christian, according to John G. Lake, a Christ-man and reveals the secret of life and communion with God through the Holy Spirit secured within our entire being.

Not without holiness

Without holiness the complete purposes of the Church cannot be fulfilled. A Holy God can only dwell in a pure vessel. John G. Lake once said, "Think not that thou shalt attain the highest in God until within thine own soul a heavenly longing to be like Him who gave His life for us possesses our own heart."[5]

Holiness and *sanctification* are sometimes used interchangeably in the Scriptures. A holy and sanctified condition can only be realized when our own fleshly nature is first revealed to us. Once the tares of our human soul are uncovered, we then call upon the grace of God to separate us from all that is ungodly and purge our spirit, soul and body from every worldly tendency.

Pursue peace with all men, and the sanctification without which no one will see the Lord.
—HEBREWS 12:14

As Lake once put it, "There arises in the heart the desire and prayer for the Spirit of God to eject, crucify and destroy every tendency of the opposition of the Holy Spirit."[6]

The heart of man must be purged by holy fire and washed from every stain by the cleansing blood of Christ.

Those who desire to be a partaker of the nature of Christ must ever feel the purging power of Christ within. Once the Holy Spirit takes up residence in us, there is a release of power through the indwelling Spirit, lifting us above the lusts and desires of this world and allowing the believer to live a holy and consecrated life.

This desire for the purity of God's nature reveals a vital ingredient in the life and ministry of John G. Lake. As he put it in 1916, "Holiness is the character of God. The very substance of His being and the essence of His nature is purity."[7] The purpose of God and the salvation of mankind is to produce in man a kindred holiness, a radiant purity like unto that of God Himself.

Clothed in a spirit of humility

Another important attribute in the ministry of Lake was his commitment to living in a spirit of humility. Lake often quoted:

> You younger men, likewise, be subject to your elders; and all of you, clothe yourselves with humility toward one another, for GOD IS OPPOSED TO THE PROUD, BUT GIVES GRACE TO THE HUMBLE.
>
> —1 PETER 5:5

If we are to return to the future, our true apostolic heritage and kingdom example, we must adhere to the qualities demonstrated by our apostolic fathers.

In Acts 20:19, the apostle Paul acknowledges his commitment to humility in his service to the Lord. The resolution to humility by the first-century apostle burned equally as bright in the heart of John Lake, a twentieth-century apostle.

Lake desired to follow the example evidenced in Moses and seek to be the most meek man in the land. By virtue of this commitment to humility, he was able to say, "the Spirit of God ran through my person like a river of heavenly fluid. Cancers withered under my touch, cripples of every type were instantly restored, and works of creation in the bodies of men took place as a result of humbling myself under the mighty hand of God."[8]

Like Moses, he desired not only to see the acts of an awesome God, but also to understand His ways. As a result, he discovered the Lord's way is through servanthood and a spirit of humility clothing the believer.

It is only through amazing grace the nature and works of Christ can be exhibited through us. God gives His grace to the humble. Humility is truly a key ingredient to the restoration of true apostolic ministry and the return of the Shekinah glory to the Church.

Alexander Dowie, a mentor of Lake, once said of humility, "In becoming an apostle, it is not a question of rising high, it is a question of becoming low enough."[9] It is not a question of becoming a Lord over God's heritage, but it is a question if a man shall be called to be an apostle whether he can get himself low enough to say from the depths of his heart as did the apostle Paul, "It is a faithful saying, worthy of all acceptance, that Jesus Christ came into this world to save sinners of whom I am chief."

The empowering presence

As with the first-century apostles, Lake would not attempt full-time ministry until he had been endued with power from on high.

Even though the early apostles had received an anointing from the Lord for casting out evil spirits and healing the sick, they had not yet become the dwelling place of God until the Day of Pentecost had fully come. It is one thing to receive anointings or gifts from the Lord, yet altogether another to become the literal dwelling place of the manifest presence of God.

Lake knew the reality of the empowering presence of God abiding within, anointing and equipping him not only to minister healing and salvation to a lost world, but also to express the radiant presence of a Holy God. As he expressed it, "Becoming a Christ-man having all the potentials through the Holy Spirit that resided in Christ Himself."[10]

His indwelling presence makes the believer a master over every power of darkness that is in the world. He is to be God's representative in the world. His presence in a Christian is to be as powerful as the Holy Spirit was in the life of Christ. Consequently, fear of evil spirits and demonic opposition is out of the question, not because of any merits of our own, but because of the Lord's dominion and victory.

Lake spent a season of prayer and fasting precisely seeking a special anointing for casting out demons. The Lord graciously responded to the request of His servant by imparting a powerful authority and boldness necessary when dealing with evil spirits. As a result, people traveled to his meetings from all over the world to be delivered and set free from demonic opposition. Tremendous testimonies are on record as evidence of this ministry.

The Lord's empowering presence also carried Lake to a substantially broadened understanding of the Scriptures. Powerful and revelatory sermons emerged from the apostle of faith as he allowed the Holy Spirit to unfold the mysteries of the kingdom. According to numerous reports, he had the capacity to inspire faith in the hearts of those who heard him.

Lake was a man without compromise when it involved the Spirit's revelation of the Word. He utterly refused to jeopardize the true revelation of the Word for a false unity that he believed resulted in spiritual weakness. He believed "principle" is better than unity, and the ultimate end of "principle" would result in the true unity of the faith as described in Ephesians 4:13.

Lake believed that the secret to Christianity is not in *doing* but in *being*—in being the possessor of the divine nature of Christ and His empowering presence. We are to be the reflection of Christ's character, and our message should be in the demonstration of the Spirit and power. It is by becoming one with the Father that we know peace in the midst of storms. It is through the Lord's abiding presence that we find the secret place of the most High and abide under the shadow of the Almighty.

Conclusion

These apostolic principles that were found in the first century Church were also demonstrated in the life of John G. Lake and are those for which we should earnestly contend. This generation has the opportunity to experience the return of our faith to that of our apostolic fathers. As we consider the days of old and the generations of long ago, we can see firsthand the application of true apostolic ministry and experience the fullness of God in this day.

SUMMARY

THE PURPOSE OF this book is to hopefully quicken desire and vision for the End-Time mandates and cooperate with the Holy Spirit in our preparation. This is perhaps the most important generation in human history with the single exception of the day of the Lord's death and resurrection. These are both sobering and exciting times requiring our full attention and sincere responses.

> But in a great house there are not only vessels of gold and silver, but also of wood and clay, some for honor and some for dishonor. Therefore if anyone cleanses himself from the latter, he will be a vessel for honor, sanctified and useful for the Master, prepared for every good work.
> —2 TIMOTHY 2:20–21 (NKJV)

The End-Time scenario is beginning to take shape and the players are starting to take their positions in the dramatic unfolding of events prophetically observed by prophets throughout history. Hunger and desire to become vessels of honor is being imparted to those given the opportunity to participate. It is our prayer that each person will respond with favor and give the Holy Spirit permission to fully clothe him with Himself, making him the instrument of His warfare and useful to the Master for every good work.

The Scriptures clearly outline, both directly and through types and shadows, the consecration and sanctification necessary to become vessels in whom the Lord will find His rest and through whom He will do His greater works. From among the various redemptive names illustrated in the Old Testament, Jehovah Shammah, "the Lord who is present," is the one with highlighted emphasis for this hour. When the promise of this redemptive name is realized, the Lord is fully present bringing with Him all of the other redemptive attributes inherent in His nature.

The Lord is our Provider, Healer, Banner, Sanctifier, Peace, Shepherd, Righteousness, Recompense, Defense (as the Lord who smites), and the Lord of Hosts, orchestrating the armies of God and providing a canopy of protection around those who are His sons and daughters. All of His attributes will be on display in amplified form during our watch.

There is a flourishing sense of anticipation and purpose in the days in which we are living. The marked increase in the intensity and focus within many Christians relates to the birthing of kingdom purposes in our nation and throughout the earth. Some individuals are beginning to experience a measure of increase in the anointing and various expressions of outpouring to quicken and prepare us for the next wave of the Spirit.

I was recently allowed by the Spirit to witness some individuals being taken "behind the veil" and shown great and mighty things that have been reserved for the End-Time.

> After these things I looked, and behold, a door standing open in heaven, and the first voice which I had heard, like the sound of a trumpet speaking with me, said, "Come up here, and I will show you what must take place after these things."
>
> —REVELATION 4:1

The objective and commission of these individuals is to

begin to understand spiritually the mysteries associated with these great truths and start the process of sharing them with the body of Christ. That is the hopeful aspiration of this book—to awaken God's people to their destiny and create desire to be groomed for their purpose.

It is our prophetic proclamation to begin to fulfill Revelation 4:1 and Jeremiah 33:3, as many saints call upon Him that He will begin to show great and awesome things which we presently do not know. The truths associated with this reality are quite significant and provide the keys that unlock prominent mysteries of the kingdom of heaven. Many of the individuals that will be allowed this experience must go through the preparation and refining described in this book that is essential for this weighty responsibility. It is difficult to adequately express the importance of being clothed with the garment of humility in the execution of this commission and the sharing of the great mysteries being imparted in this hour.

As the experience continued, the Holy Spirit revealed how the sharing of kingdom truths with the body of Christ was likened to the preparation of a great banqueting table being set for the Lord and His Bride. Seemingly, the "implements and banners" that were being revealed to this group somehow were utilized in the adornment of the banqueting table, particularly around the area that was clearly recognized as the "seat of honor." Naturally, these things are shown in symbolic form to illustrate truth that will help us in the hour in which we are living and the responsibility being delegated to us by the Holy Spirit.

One of the banners that was emphasized depicted a picture of the High Priest in all of his adornment with the breastplate, golden miter and other garments. When the banner was displayed, a voice spoke with clarity and determined purpose and stated, "My banner over you is love."

> Like an apple tree among the trees of the forest, so is
> my beloved among the young men. In his shade I
> took great delight and sat down, and his fruit was
> sweet to my taste. He has brought me to his banquet
> hall, and his banner over me is love.
>
> —SONG OF SOLOMON 2:3–4

There will be many who will be allowed to go behind the
veil, to obtain and experience expressions of His divine love
that will transcend anything that we presently know. It will
be a greater comprehension of His love and heavenly design
for this generation and a fulfillment of John 17:26, that we
may love Him with the love wherewith the Father did love
Him. His love for us will supply the essential spiritual provisions necessary to see us through to our promises.

This central truth is an emphasis of the Holy Spirit
pointing us to a form of genuine unity with Him that will
also birth in us brotherly love and fraternal affection.
Jealousy and selfish ambition have no place in the joining of
individuals and ministries for the purpose of pursuing a
higher mandate and greater fruitfulness during the End-
Time generation. Throughout the church there is an aligning
of people and ministries that will produce a much higher
anointing and authority in the realm of the Spirit.

One need only look at the evening news to discern that
the hour in which we are living clearly points to the many
biblical prophecies foretelling and describing a day of profound significance. Just as the Bible describes, all things are
being shaken so that those things that remain can stand
under the scrutiny and pressure of the harvest generation.

The prophet Zechariah foretells a unique day that is
known only to the Lord and is neither day nor night—a day

in which light and darkness become apparent at the same time. This will be quite a significant day in which individuals will become the light of the world displaying the bright and virtuous attributes of God Himself.

> **And it will come about in that day that there will be no light; the luminaries will dwindle. For it will be a unique day which is known to the LORD, neither day nor night, but it will come about that at evening time there will be light.**
>
> **—ZECHARIAH 14:6–7**

This day is so remarkable that only the Holy Spirit can make ready a company of people to meet the challenges and spiritual demands of this hour. As it is written, "at evening time it shall be light." This is the "evening time" of human history and the light of God is about to shine.

Many of the events that have taken place throughout history have provided a rehearsal for the confrontation between light and darkness as the Holy Spirit orchestrates the training of His army. Likewise, our adversary is also providing polluted authority to those who have set themselves in opposition to the Lord Jesus and His End-Time mandates.

Clearly, there are many purposes for which we are being equipped and prepared. However, three notable divine mandates begin to emerge as our primary focus. Our highest purpose and the one instrumental in allowing us to achieve all other purposes and mandates, is to know God as personally and intimately as He may be known. There is an open door and a call to come up higher to a place of fellowship and exchange with the Creator and establish friendship with God.

From that place of communion we begin to receive the unveiling of His nature and attributes that are not merely intellectual perceptions but revelation and comprehension of

His person. The prophet Isaiah was given the great privilege of seeing heaven's design before the throne of God as seraphim spoke one to another declaring, "Holy, Holy, Holy is the Lord of hosts" (Isaiah 6:3). They were allowed to see with their eyes demonstrations of His majesty and authority and give expression to it. Their words began to fill the temple with smoke and glory by witnessing with their eyes and expressing with their lips the revelation of God sitting upon His throne in absolute and perfect supremacy and sovereignty.

As the seraphim gave glory to Him and He received the glory due Him, more of his divine attributes began to be revealed causing an even greater expression of praise and glory. This kingdom exchange and heavenly design continued filling the atmosphere with the glory and illumination of God until the entire temple was saturated with the appearance and revelation of His glory. That is the fashion of heaven that is to be transferred to the earth and a second End-Time mandate to create an atmosphere on the earth that is consistent with His nature and character in which He can dwell.

If we can fulfill this mandate, all the other purposes and desires for which we long will naturally be established and achieved by His presence and anointing resting in us. We must likewise become the instruments that create a similar atmosphere on earth so He can tabernacle among us and accomplish all that He has foretold for this generation.

The third mandate for winning the lost and healing the sick will inherently take place because of the evident glory of God resting on the Lord's friends because of the close encounters they have with Him. We are given the incredible opportunity in this generation to function under the principles of the kingdom of heaven and experience intimacy with God and demonstrate the power of the age to come.

NOTES

Introduction
1. Charles H. Spurgeon, *Spurgeon's Expository Encyclopedia* (Grand Rapids, MI: Baker Books, 1977), n.p.

Chapter 1
1. John G. Lake and Kenneth Copeland, *John G. Lake: His Life, His Sermons, His Boldness of Faith* (Fort Worth: Kenneth Copeland Publications, 1996), n.p.

Chapter 6
1. Gordon Lindsay, *John Alexander Dowie* (Dallas, TX: Christ for the Nations, 1986), n.p.

Chapter 11
1. M. B. Woodworth and Maria Woodworth-Etter, *A Diary of Signs and Wonders* (Tulsa, OK: Harrison House, 1981), n.p.
2. Ibid.

Chapter 16
1. Lindsay, *John Alexander Dowie.*

Chapter 18
1. Lake and Copeland, *John G. Lake: His Life, His Sermons, His Boldness of Faith.*
2. Ibid.
3. Ibid.
4. Ibid.
5. Ibid.
6. Ibid.
7. Ibid.
8. Ibid.
9. Lindsay, *John Alexander Dowie.*
10. Lake and Copeland, *John G. Lake: His Life, His Sermons, His Boldness of Faith.*

Contact the author at:

WHITEDOVE MINISTRIES

P. O. Box 1634
Orange Beach, AL 36561
http://www.whitedoveministries.org

251-1FHK
www.fhkfc.org